A Surfing Adventure in the Mentawai Islands

Clive M. Woodward

# DEDICATION

To fellow surfers, adventurers and armchair explorers everywhere.

# FOREWARD

"The reader will observe that Clive is not just a humble diarist and waterman, but also a raconteur, poet, philosopher, romantic and comedian all rolled into one.

He got into the water for the first session first – the rest of us "frothers" had thought we had to wait for the engine to stop to jump in. OK, so this guy had done his prep and was serious. But could a Tassie boy, sporting an anaemic librarian's suntan, cope hour after hour under the equatorial sun? Surely my Queensland upbringing would provide a decisive advantage.

By day 6, Clive was out of reach. He'd surfed more hours than I thought was humanly possible and none of us had any way of catching him. Clive was always on the first dinghy at dawn each morning and then just didn't get out of the water. By the fourth day, his eyes looked scary, like he had accidentally put hydrochloric acid in them. His campaign was one of monumental preparation, application and endurance never before witnessed in Indonesian waters. The rest of us looked on in breathless admiration.

On the last morning, the rain came pouring down and the surf disappeared. We all watched nervously from the boat. Clive was sitting in a non-existent line up in heavy rain on his own. The skipper was anxious to leave to avoid a storm that was brewing for the crossing back to Padang. We watched and we waited and we watched some more. In the final hour Clive didn't even paddle for a wave because there was none to catch (despite his later recollections to the contrary). Eventually, after much discussion and consultation, tour leader Deano made a humane call and sent the dinghy to pick him up. It was surfing's equivalent of a mercy killing.

The account which follows is destined to become a literary epic and best seller."

Doug - fellow traveller

A Surfing Adventure In The Mentawai Islands

# CONTENTS

# ACKNOWLEDGMENTS

I thank my fellow tour members for their companionship and good humour, the crew of The Addiction for being knowledgeable and gracious hosts and the people of the Mentawai Islands for accepting our presence in their waters.

The Author at HTs

A Surfing Adventure In The Mentawai Islands

# 1. TUBES AND TIGER CLAWS

Surfing the majestic HTs, one of the world's most perfect and photogenic surf breaks, is akin to being seduced by a beautiful, scantily clad vampire temptress. You are drawn in by her seductive curves and allure, despite knowing all is not as it seems. Then just as you look deep into her eyes and her lips pout for a first kiss, she draws back her lips and bares her teeth.

Of course, in truth, the surf break has no malice or evil intent. She is more a sculptress than temptress who, for centuries, has been impassively carving exquisite liquid artwork awaiting an appreciative audience. It just so happens that her tools of trade are razor sharp.

After endlessly repeating her outdoor exhibition through the ages, largely ignored by local villagers, finally in 1990 her talent was understood when Lance Knight, a Mentawai surfing pioneer, rode into the bay with a local fisherman in a dugout canoe. He watched awestruck as liquid mounds rose up out of the ocean into cobra hooded peaks and spilled over in elliptical blue arcs that ran down the reef towards him. He had discovered every surfer's fantasy wave. Lance sampled her works in private for weeks on his own, living in the small village hidden in the palm lined cove.

Eventually, the sculptress became famous and her work an object of desire across the surfing world.

From a distance the break is a vision of heaven.

Shimmering aqua-blue waves peel in perfect symmetry across the reef into the deep channel. The potential danger is masked by the aqua blue water and photogenic quality of the wave set in an idyllic palm fringed bay. Once close to the break, however, it begins to look more serious as you can sense the power and the sinister sight of a slab of reef periodically sucking dry draws your gaze. It is not until you are in the line-up, paddling for a fast moving peak looking down the wave face to the grinning teeth of the reef below, that your mouth puckers dry and you fully realize that the wave is a serious hazard to your health.

*  *  *

This knowledge was tucked away in the back of my mind as I stepped out of the cool upper deck cabin into the tropical warmth of the first morning of my Mentawai surfing adventure. Outwardly calm, I was nonetheless alive with a sense of anticipation. A tantalising ten days of chasing perfect waves on the isolated coral reefs stretched ahead.

Despite being a surf veteran having started surfing way back in 1973, I was far from a jaded, world weary surf traveller. The always cool, and often freezing, waters of Tasmania were, and are still, my typical surfing fare. My first belated experience of Indonesian perfection had been a long time coming in these very same islands only two years before. I had been excited then but was even more so on this trip.

I now knew that I could handle most of the waves on offer and was better prepared after building up my fitness and having a steady diet of whatever surf I could squeeze into weekends in the lead up to the expedition.

Even professional surfers, whose lives are a blur of travel and amazing waves, get excited about trips to the Mentawais. For me, the treats of such a trip were many. The attractions were heightened by their novelty. Cruising the tropics was a chance to visit imagined scenes from various South Pacific tales I had read avidly and lived vicariously over the years. Warm water was a luxury in itself. But, the prospect of catching more quality waves on the tour than would ever come my way in years back home was what really stoked the furnace of my excitement. In the modern surf vernacular, I was "frothing".

My excitement was mildly peppered with unease. Inevitably I was going to end up in some dangerous situations in the coming weeks, riding the fine line between fun and disaster that surfing over sharp coral reefs entails.

I stood on the lower deck taking everything in. The ocean was a patchwork of wind ruffles amongst oily-smooth expanses of pure glass. Occasionally, a smattering of silver flashes would spread in unison across the water as small flying fish raced to escape an unseen predator. Our twin hulled catamaran, The Addiction, sliced through the water with a sense of purpose. A barely perceptible roll from what little swell managed to squeeze through the gaps between the islands to the west hinted at the possibilities for surf later that morning.

Off to the right, a pile of board bags lay stacked high waiting to be unpacked. A huge bunch of finger-sized bananas hung off the roof ready for a quick snack between surfs. Some old yellowed and battered surfboards, veterans of many a trip, were strung up high in the rafters next to two sleek newer ones - clearly the Skipper's quiver. A few well thumbed surfing magazines sat pinned to the table by a large Conch Shell. It was definitely not another day at the office.

A few of the guys were also on deck, no-one saying much, just enjoying the morning and looking towards the distant green smudge on the horizon. Our tour members were an interesting mix of old mates from back in my teenage surfing days and some new acquaintances. We were all drawn together by Dean, the six foot two, 120 kg, and surprisingly athletic, fifty one year old man-mountain tour leader.

I stepped down into the cool of the main cabin for breakfast. It was spacious with an open kitchen area, a long dining table and, at the far end, a line of couches fronting a large plasma television. A water cooler stood by the edge of the kitchen and a refrigerator full of ice cold soft drinks over by the wall. The mouth watering waft of pancakes hung in the air as Tony, the hard working cook, was already preparing a hot breakfast.

We certainly were not roughing it.

\* \* \*

Our adventure was not to be anything similar to the
experiences of the early explorers and missionaries in
the islands of the Pacific that I loved to read about,
where heat, thirst, disease, shipwrecks, typhoons and
dangerous encounters with the native islanders often
made for tortuous journeys and great armchair reading.
Our adventures would begin once we leapt over the side
of the boat armed, not with a cutlass or pistol, but with a
delicately foiled surfboard.

Surfing can be playful but has many more mini-
adventures and intense experiences than would be
apparent to the casual observer. A heavy take-off over a
shallow reef can become a lifetime memory burned by
the laser of fear. A perfect wave can feel as though you
are flying, swooping birdlike through aqua blue glassy
power pockets. A wipe-out can blast you across the
reef, tumbling out of control only a metre or so above
sharp coral. A friend can disappear into the maelstrom
of broken waves to reappear ten minutes later, shaken
and wide eyed, mumbling about a long hold down and a
narrow escape on the inside reef where a thin layer of
water lay between soft unprotected skin and live coral.

When experienced surfers get together to share stories,
they always have a wealth of tales to tell. Travel is a big
part of surfing and many tales revolve around the
journey, not the waves. But, when the talk turns to
riding waves and wipeouts, although the dramas are
measured in seconds or a few minutes at most, the
events are still intense and memorable.

This tale of travel and adventures seeks to capture both

the dramatic and the simple pleasures of days spent away from the cares of the world hunting waves in a location as exotic and alluring as any that exists on this earth.

* * *

Over breakfast, my sense of calm was eroded more than a little when half way through a well filled bowl of muesli, the Skipper popped his head through the cabin door and laconically informed in his American accent that we were heading straight for HTs. The shallow reef at HTs has left many a tiger claw scrape on highly competent surfers. The apt naming of the inside shelf at the end of the wave as The Surgeons Table, added to the spot's ability to intimidate.

The Skipper had grown up in Hawaii surfing the powerful open ocean peaks of Sunset Beach as his regular spot. He had also spent years in Indonesia surfing the heaviest waves across the archipelago. The Skipper later confessed to us that that he felt he had a sort of understanding with HTs where he treated her well and she was kind to him in return. For him, dropping into HTs for a surf was just another day at the office. But for us, the name summoned up visions of the ultimate surfing fantasy perfection tinged with a strong sense of dread.

HTs was my nemesis on my first trip to the Mentawais – an adventure that was part surf trip and part reunion of old surfing mates. At the ripe old age of 49 I had lost some weight, rebuilt my paddle strength and signed up for the trip of a lifetime. Fickle surf in the lead up to the trip meant that I missed the essential surf time preparation needed to move from waist high beach breaks to serious coral reef surf spots with any sort of comfort.

Five minutes into my first surf and I was in caught inside by a non stop set of powerful 6 foot waves at what was termed a "soft spot" questioning how I would cope with 10 days of this. It took a few days to adjust.

In the end, I had a very enjoyable trip surfing a wide variety of spots but to our unspoken horror the Skipper kept taking us back to HTs whenever the wind swung in from the west. On the final visit he noticed some huge swells building as we headed up the coast from Macaronis (where I would have been very content to stay another day) and leaned down from the upper deck to give some words of advice,

> "There's some huge sets coming through boys, you had better get your survival skills ready".

That was enough for some of the tour members. They pulled their cameras out of their bags ready to record the drama and left their boards untouched. I quietly asked him what he meant by "survival skills". He laid out a few hints,

> "Don't catch the first waves of the set, you'll get slammed by the rest if you blow it. If you wipe out just swim for the horizon as fast as you can – don't pull your board in first, you'll waste precious seconds that could help you escape the next wave".

After that exchange, the mood of those determined to try to catch a few of these monsters took on the solemn tension of soldiers preparing for battle.

The Skipper certainly made sure we had photos to prove he found us perfect waves. However, solid overhead HTs was not really something we were prepared for. Most of the guys just watched from the boat. I somewhat reluctantly had four surfs there all up and left with the noteworthy result of having only one wipe-out on a medium sized day across all four trips to the line up – a feat made a little less impressive by my measly tally of about fifteen waves all up. I was careful and treated every take-off with total focus.

Everywhere else in the Mentawais we surfed was fun once I settled in to the various line-ups. I caught heaps of waves and spent long hours in the water, but HTs left me with a sense of unfinished business. This feeling grew each time I looked at our photos and videos of perfect tubes peeling off its reef. They looked so tame on film which totally hid what lay feet below the surface!

* * *

The Addiction was eating up the miles at a surprising pace. The distant line of green islands now had definition. A ubiquitous line of coconut palms underlined by a strip of white sandy beach was clearly visible.

Activity on board shifted into a higher gear quickly as soon as we realised that the surf would be only ten minutes away at this speed. Boards were unpacked, fins screwed in and board shorts, booties and rash vests dug out of bags with a sense of urgency. Looking around, Taff was a familiar sight getting things sorted with a serious look on his face. I noted new friends Doug, Charlie and Dave were looking pretty intense too and well prepared. They were fit, had new boards, the latest fin systems and a pre-trip reputation for getting in the surf early and catching a lot of waves. Taff and I tended to be the early birds on the last trip but would have some company and competition this time.

I kept glancing up in between sorting out my gear and waxing my board. All I could see at first was what looked like an innocent trickle of white water swinging around the inside of the island and heading north. The reefs fringing the edge of the island somehow manage to bend the swell lines around almost 180 degrees without losing much height, creating a surf spot on the sheltered inside of the island where surf should not really break at all. Westerly winds from the open ocean blow off the land producing clean conditions when many other spots along the island chain are blown out.

It looked very small and mellow from a distance. The deck was soon a mess of unzipped board bags, packing materials and freshly waxed boards. Not much was said. Dean's preparations were typically more leisurely. Paul and Tim were getting gear ready but checking it all out a bit more carefully to see if the conditions would suit them. Hoover was understandably looking pissed off as his boards and gear were somewhere in Sumatra, perhaps never to be seen again after the travel dramas of the day before.

I was ready to hit the water as we swung into the bay and finally had a close look at an empty line up. A single shoulder high wave peeled down the reef looking lots of fun and not serious at all. Hell, it even looked like a fun beach break – not the thundering peaks I had seen two years before when, late on the evening of the big day, a twenty wave set poured into the bay exploding with a bone jarring crack after crack in the stillness of the dusk.

"Inconsistent" I thought to myself and very manageable –even just plain fun. It also looked a bit too good to be true. Empty, sunny, offshore, no boats, no local kids surfing the end section, and no one on the beach it seemed. Mostly in surfing you just can't take empty waves for granted. "Grab them while you can", is the often hard-learned lesson. Even in the remote Mentawais, a boat full of surfers can turn up at any time or six tanned, fit young wave hogs could come strolling out of the jungle from their afternoon nap when least expected.

I was off the boat and paddling hard straight away driven by wanting to get a few good waves before something came to break the spell. Taff, Doug, Dave, Pete and Charlie were close behind. Dean followed soon after. I had taken my short fish style board out as it really did look like a slightly wind ruffled beach break on a sunny morning.

My arms felt strong and powerful as I cut through the water. The water was warm and softly textured as it flowed across my chest and legs, in sharp contrast to the cool, dense sea on my last surf in far off Tasmania. The line-up ahead was devoid of waves during a lull between sets and looked like an innocuous blue swimming pool.

I found my spot in the line-up midway along the reef according to my couch-concocted plan. I was inside everyone else so had taken a step towards going for it more and chasing the "mega HT barrel" – hopefully with a photo for proof (Geni, the on-board photographer, had set up the tender in the channel and was shooting stills). The tide was fairly low - hence the lack of crowd we realised later, as many surfers will not surf it through the low tide because it is too shallow for comfort. Some waves rolled through and I studied where and how they hit the reef.

The furthest inside take-off zone looked ugly. A few coral heads were sticking out of the water right in front of where the inside peak pops up sometimes. The description "coral head' was exactly right in their case. They were as if some ancient tribe had buried some of their enemies neck-deep in the coral leaving only their round heads exposed to become encrusted with coral. They waited patiently ready to slice unfortunate surfers or to entangled their legropes in a death grip.

Deep inside off the edge of the shallowest wedge of reef the waves peeled perfectly at times right across the reef to the channel giving theoretically a tube of incredible length and intensity. From where I sat though the dangers were all too apparent. Just after the peaks heaved over and began their spinning path across the reef the exploding white water paused for a second as its energy went upwards, before surging forward with a roar over the reef's edge with the full power of a recently broken wave. When the ocean drew back between waves it drained off a wall of live coral. The peaks also swung into different spots with each set, a bit like a beach break, making wave judgment critical. Being caught over on the inside would be more than awkward. It would be too shallow to duck dive anything. The only option would be to get washed up onto the reef and hope for the best. The reef's edge looked jagged and undercut suggesting a slam into its serrated teeth would be more likely than being swept over it to calmer water in the lagoon that fringed the beach.

Any plans to go right over to the far inside takeoff spot to get the 100 metre barrel of the trip, as I had daydreamed of doing back home on the couch, were quickly shelved. So I sat cautiously on the edge of the second peak, safer, but still well in harm's way if things went astray. At 51, I was a competent and a reasonably agile surfer but shoulder high beach breaks were my bread and butter. Pulling into low tide HT barrels was not familiar territory at all.

Very few waves were coming through initially and it took a while to get my first wave. I am not sure who caught the first wave of the trip but think it was either Doug or Dave. A few head high sets had passed already and I had been slightly out of position for what was a very precise take off. If you were not in the spot it would suck out underneath you and throw you over the falls into what appeared to be waist deep water. I sat there gazing at the horizon and alternatively at the reef below – a mass of colour from the live coral contrasting with my very un-tropical white legs. In the distance, the sliver of white sand fringed the palm tree lined shore in the tranquil bay. The curve of the reef somehow concentrated all the swell energy onto the reef we were surfing leaving the inner bay calm, peaceful and inviting. All this created a strange juxtaposition of tranquility with lurking danger.

Finally, a solid wave came through and I paddled hard. The take-off went from straight-forward to very steep immediately and I ended up going out onto the flats a fair way with the sheer speed of the drop. By the time I looked up it was starting to zip away down the line with me yet to bottom turn. In that split second I rightly, or wrongly, pictured my turn being too late and envisioned getting the lip right on the head if I tried to pull in. The reef seemed very close to my left. The advice of "if you wipe-out at HTs do it early so you don't get pushed in too far" was imprinted on my brain. My lack of familiarity with pulling into serious fast tubes over coral became painfully obvious. So I dived hard through the back for a minor tumble and popped up a little shaken wondering if I had just missed a fantastic barrel or a nasty drag over the reef. I was annoyed with myself for hesitating and even more so when I repeated the same thing on my next wave. My old mate Dean helpfully suggested I pull in next time. My third wave was medium sized and I made it easily. Things were looking up. My dreams of the mega barrel at HTs might just happen.

Then the tempo of the whole surf then shifted into a

different, much more intense gear with the arrival of a set almost double the size of anything we had seen so far. We all spotted it swinging into the outer corner of the reef and put our heads down and paddled like mad to get over it. We all just made it. As I pushed through the top I glanced across at the huge grinding tube steaming towards me drawing water off the reef leaving a thin veneer of transparent glass over the coral below. I was once again shocked at the power, grace and authority of HTs.

A hint of double up comes into play on the bigger sets from the outside reef focusing the swell and muscling the wave up into something unlike any other spot I have surfed. With almost no wind, the sets were translucent walls of clear gelatin, flavoured by red and green coral. The vision as I looked along the line of the big sets to the channel was of a fluid sculpture heaving itself out of the depths into a wall of molten glass. After it drew to full height it paused for a brief moment then threw majestically over into an elliptical tube. The sculptress was putting on a special performance.

The huge grizzly bear had just confronted the admiring weekend hiker. It had gone up on its hind legs to full height, puffed out its chest and fur and looked him straight in the eye. In that instant, I knew I was partly beaten. I was not going to go anywhere near that inside take off. I was also questioning if I could swing around and take one of the biggest sets at all.

My shift in mood made some sense. This was no longer the playful shoulder high wave I first spotted as we entered the bay. With the whole Indian Ocean out there generating swell trains heading for the Mentawais, who knew what might be about to happen if a strong pulse from a distant storm came through?

I had visions of experiencing a reef drag on the first day of the trip cutting me up and sending me back to the boat to nurse my wounds. I did not fancy spending 10 days on the boat fending off infections unable to make the most of the waves to come. One guide to the Mentawais on a surf travel website said of HTs "go there later in the trip when you are surfing well and so it won't ruin the trip if you get cut up". My caution was clearly warranted.

HTs' set up gives the sense that when riding a wave or if caught inside that the waves are pushing you straight towards trouble. It hits the reef fairly squarely and the Surgeon's Table hooks around at the end closing the escape to the channel. Some other nearby spots such as Macaronis, Lances Lefts and Thunders are shallow but except for the most inside take-offs they push *down* the reef. You have the sense that generally, if you paddle hard sideways, you can get out of the shallow area quickly. HTs feels like you are skateboarding down a ramp towards a brick wall. If you stuff it up, the angles are all wrong to avoid a bad situation.

The big set left us all a bit rattled. Where to sit became an issue – inside for medium ones risking getting caught inside or to take on a big set? The decisions were not the casual choice of where to sit on some sandy beach break back home. They would have consequences. Last trip, Taff had been caught well inside by a huge set and was swept into the shallows where his legrope became caught around a coral head. He tried to pull the release on the Velcro around his ankle but was being bashed around and could not get a grip on it. He remained tightly fastened deep under water in a scary situation for a long time. Eventually Taff managed to get it off but not before a final indignity from a local trigger fish that zoomed out of a crevice in the reef and bit him on the bum.

Another big set came through. I paddled over a couple of huge, steep, glassy walls that I could have caught that would have rated, if I had caught them, as the most dramatic and scary waves of my entire surfing career. He chance had passed Dean quietly say to me,

> "Clive, you need to say if you are not going for a wave, I could have caught that one".

> "Classic gutsy Dean" I thought to myself, "I'm freaking out and he is trying to catch the damn things".

We settled down a bit. Waves were ridden by all the guys in between paddles over the top of some big sets. I remember Taff getting a good one and seeing a squirt of spray over the back of the wave as he came off the top. Others were paddling out after waves regularly. Tim had come off the boat into the channel to watch from up close. He was an old mate from way back who that was worse the wear from decades of being a deckhand lifting huge craypots out on the heaving Western Australian swells. These days, back and neck problems and a major deterioration in eyesight, to the point where he was classed as legally blind, restricted him to the smaller days. But his love of the surf drew him off the boat into the channel for a close-up view of one of the greatest sights on earth – perfect HTs.

Up to this point, I think the biggest sets still went un-ridden. No-one claimed any that night over beers. For normally desk bound middle aged surfers they were simply too intimidating for the first surf of the trip.

We had noticed a few figures in on the beach in the shade of the coconut palms watching the waves for the past half hour or so - patiently waiting for the tide to fill in a bit. On the horizon a couple of other charter boats had also come in to view heading our way. Our "mates only" session was about to be disturbed.

Before long, two young tanned French guys arrived having paddled off the beach and took claim of the inside take-off spot. They had the bleached hair and deep tans that spoke of a long Indonesian sojourn. We found out later that they had been staying at the bay for over a month surfing every day and were very familiar with the wave. They went straight for the big sets without hesitation. A few of their take-offs were big but "easy" where the peak let them in and they could bottom turn into the slot. Quite a few, however, required a really quick turn jammed in the face halfway down to set up the tube and avoid getting too far out onto the flat of the waves, as I had done on my first two waves, before bottom turning as the rate of peel was just too fast to lose precious seconds.

Technically this is one of the more subtle and difficult moves in surfing. In heavy reef waves it is often necessary to make the wave but flirts with danger. A slight misjudged pressure by toes on the inside rail of the board could pop out the inside fin, leaving the surfer to fall flat on their face mid-way down the wave. From there the flow of water would be still moving vertically, drawing the surfer up to the wave's crest buried in the lip. Then the wave will throw them over into space body lengths down to the wave's trough. The landing spot would be the shallowest spot where the wave had drawn all the water off the reef. Momentum alone would then drive them deep, with an extra push from the thick lip increasing the force behind the plunge. Contact with coral is a likely outcome.

All too soon other boats arrived. The crowd grew. The hunt for waves became harder and more competitive. All of the Addiction crew except me went back to the boat for a break. By this time I had caught about 8 waves. I made every take-off but I had taken around four wipe-outs and finally knew what it was like to be tumbled shoreward at running speed over the famous reef hoping that the coral just below did not hit me. The safe zone was only a chest deep layer of water. Somehow it was just enough.

Even though I dislike crowds, especially in heavy waves, I was reluctant to end my surf just yet. I stayed out and began to pick off some very good waves. I did not ride any deep tubes but enjoyed a series of speed runs across perfect walls with the reef rushing by below, magnified into exquisite details of coral ledges by the lens effect of the curves of the wave. One wave felt like I was riding rock rather than water as a ridge of coral seemed to stick up into the wave in a line with me flying above it. There was a certain magic point just after the take-off when I knew I was in the right spot to make the wave and could set my line is the power zone and then weave up and down enjoying the sense of speed and weightlessness.

* * *

Surfing is a huge amalgam of experiences and sensations that extend well beyond what happens in the water. At the heart of everything, of course, lies riding waves. This apparently simple act has, in itself, a multitude of dimensions and a wide spectrum of extremes on the pleasure scale. In poor quality waves, surfing can be as mundane as eating breakfast or walking your dog. Perfect waves are as exciting and mind-blowing as any experience a human can have on this earth. At its core, the thrill of surfing waves has sensations best understood to the non-surfer in terms of the feelings we associate with speed, acceleration and flying. A study by designers of amusement park roller coasters once found that some of the most enjoyable sections of the ride were not the sheer drops or ridiculous tight turns. Rather, they were the stretches in between where the passengers went through a sequence of small climbs and dips creating smooth weightless moments at speed, each with subtle shifts in acceleration – the exact same pattern of moves surfers repeat when riding good waves.

Climbing and dropping along a fast moving wall of water feels like a form of flight. It is those rare and savoured dreams of flying like a bird brought to reality. The sense of speed is magnified by the closeness of the wave's face as it whizzes past often only inches away from your eyes. Speed sensations are also felt through your feet by the direct physical connection to the wave's power source provided by the thin sliver of surfboard. A shift in weight, heel or toe pressure generates an immediate response in speed and direction. Powerful waves like HTs place a miniature jet engine beneath your feet squirting out pulses of speed at your command.

The sensation of flight becomes most real in very fast hollow waves that are clean and glassy - removing any hint through bump or board chatter that you are a not actually airborne. On a few waves I rode at HTs that morning I left gravity and human form behind and swooped for a few precious moments bird-like at eye-watering speed encased in a moving glass tube.

Peak moments in surfing are always brief and transitory. Rides are measured in seconds before the hunt begins for the next ride. In between waves there is often another mix of visual and textural pleasures. There are other waves to watch, the scenery to behold and the warmth of the sun to savour. Paddling out after a good wave past quality waves spinning past is a visual feast in itself.

A whole surf fashion industry has been built on the foundations of the dramatic visual backdrop surfing provides. Professional surfers in the latest short designs stand tall in the deep blue caverns of tropical waves.

A good surf is much more than just the sum of the cumulative seconds spent riding waves.

* * *

Wipe-outs and crowds are usually the spell breakers. Late in the surf, reality came rushing back when I dropped in on a muscle-bound Frenchman thinking he had no chance to make it around a long section in the wave. I was forced to do a quick exit straight up and out of the wave when I caught a glimpse of him behind me. This caused some brief tension as he paddled directly for me, gave me the stare and bulked up his huge shoulders. He pointed out in a mix of English and French that this was a serious wave and dropping in was very "dangereux". I apologised profusely. It provided the boys back on the boat some entertainment as they had a ringside seat of a rather angry Frenchman and a possible impending punch up.

The Frenchman's revenge occurred sometime later on my last wave when another guy from his boat did not even check inside and dropped in on me. I straightened out, quickly jumped off backwards and let the broken wave pass over. Suddenly, I was in a spot of bother. So far, mostly the sets had only a couple of waves making an escape back out through the break easy enough. Just my luck, this one had about eight overhead waves yet to come through. I was well and truly in the impact zone and paddled hard, duck diving row after row of white water as I was being pushed steadily towards the infamous Surgeon's Table coral shelf. I could see it sucking dry not far away and with each dive I was edging ever closer.

My dives were shallow to avoid going head first into the coral meaning I took the full force of each successive white water explosion head on. Out of the corner of my eye, between dives, I could see the guys on our boat, cold juices in hand, safely watching my predicament from only 50 metres away. My plan was no plan. All I could do was battle on. If I was dragged over the reef I would have to react by instinct to keep legs and arms out of harm's way or perhaps let my board take the beating and somehow bounce over into the deep water.

Soon enough I was almost on the reef and saw, from close up, the muscled back of a wave as it crunched down on dry coral. Duck diving again, I popped up expecting a final tackle from the endless set to throw me to my doom. It was not to be. The set had finally stopped. Mother Nature had made her point. I paddled exhausted into the channel and sat there in deep water for a while recovering my breath. I took the hint and paddled back for some food and rest on the boat.

Back on board everyone was eating, drinking, smoking, reading or watching the surf as suited tastes and states of mind. Hoover was sound asleep on the top bunk of our cabin after making a brief appearance for breakfast. He was clearly making the most of every moment.

Dean was also having a snooze relishing living for a while away from deadlines and endless travel around the country working on development deals.

My drop in had been a highlight of the morning for the

observers on the boat, especially as they saw the French guy's huge over muscled shoulders hunch up in anger as he headed my way. Perversely, another favourite event for those watching had been my recent struggle and escape from the clutches of The Surgeons Table. We are all not so far removed from the ancient Romans watching gladiators do battle enjoying misfortune.

The general sense of the boat was that we had had some good waves but were not quite ready for sizeable HTs on our first day. Doug and Dean had not even surfed since their last trip a year ago! For them, commitments and crowds had forced surfing into an intense annual event rather than a weekend ritual.

I sat on deck next to Tim and watched some waves peel by. The setting was amazing. Tropical blue walls lined up across the reef and span towards us – sometimes empty and sometimes with a spec of human hitching a ride. The end of the wave was only metres away from where the boat was moored in the deep channel. We could watch one of the greatest shows on earth with an ice cold orange juice in hand.

Sometimes it was a connoisseur's appreciative observation of the skills of one of the two young French guys dropping into a massive peak from way inside. Occasionally it was the more sadistic opportunity to watch an unfortunate surfer caught inside, struggling to either sneak out the back again or deal with the awkward process of being swept up on the reef.

The whole place was amazing – a freak of nature. The perfection of the wave was matched by picture postcard setting of the bay.

Two years before on a calm day I had dived around the area in amongst the live coral and along the cliff like edge of the reef. In the deep spots in the channel, delicate large brown dishes of fan coral sat unperturbed by the nearby explosions. Underwater it was beautiful and peaceful. I expected a very even, flat bottom to mirror the clean lines of the waves above. This was not the case at all. The jagged edges and unevenness of the reef gave no hint that it could produce such perfect waves from waist high to triple overhead. Overall, the macro angles and slope of the reef were what mattered and contoured the waves just so. However, the shelving slopes were not smooth and even. They were cut across with channels, edges and ledges just waiting to catch an unlucky foot or leg.

By this time the crowd was also growing and with three boats at anchor with ten or so surfers on each, the prospect of crowded, if perfect, HTs for the rest of the day was not very appealing. If you have the guts to paddle right inside any wave is yours but hassling on the middle take off spot in heavy waves could be frustrating. Talk turned to Lances Lefts further around the southern corner of island in the hope that the wave would be less crowded.

Unknown to us all, at that very point, the master investment strategist, Skelts, was down in his cabin secretly plotting a takeover bid for the position of top dog of the 2012 tour. He had carefully planned a sneaky second session whilst his fellow tour members were

distracted with food and sleep. Skelts had worded up
The Addiction's cook to serve an early lunch to the rest
of us as a distraction to facilitate his casual stroll onto
deck and leap over the side for his second surf minus at
least a few competitors for waves.

Meanwhile, musing on the possibilities Lances Lefts an
hour's motor away became firm plans all of a sudden,
with the Skipper being led a bit too much by some
Mentawai novices ignorant of just how protected we
were from a stiff westerly wind in the bay at HTs.  Later,
Charlie, as a good CEO should, took all the blame for
the decision, but Taff and I were more involved than we
ever let on.  It made no sense really to be motoring away
from perfect offshore HTs towards probably onshore
Lances Lefts but optimism and mobility can be fickle
companions.

Skelts had been in his cabin finishing off his
preparations for his sting mission.  He would sneak out
whilst everyone was eating and grab a set wave from
way inside and get a huge stand up barrel.  Geni would
get the shot of the trip with him standing tall in the tube
with dry hair perfectly in place.

Friendly competition sat as amusing undercurrents
throughout the trip.  Doug and Charlie, in particular,
seemed to have an ongoing rivalry. Mostly it seemed
surf related as far as I could see.  Coops mentioned once
that they virtually counted waves and I could imagine
them heading back to their cabins after each surf to tally
up their respective waves, tubes and drop ins in little
battered notebooks full of similar counts from

numerous past trips.

Upon hearing the motor start, Skelts emerged from his cabin with steam coming out of his ears and a look of incredulity stamped on his face. He was very pissed off. His secret plan was foiled. He also thought it ridiculous that we were breaking the cardinal rule of surfing "never leave good surf unless you are totally surfed out or very confident that better waves were to be found". Skelts looked around for a guilty party to blame as we motored out and around another set of perfect waves and into the teeth of a stiffening westerly wind. I settled down to lunch and tried to look unassuming, innocent and pre-occupied with food.

The wind began to look uglier after we moved out of the bay and the waves rolling under the boat grew the further we went towards Lance's Lefts. We had moved out of the lee of the island into open ocean swells. Surf prospects were dimming quickly and my guilt at having a hand in a bad decision affecting a boatload of on edge surfers increased with each mile. Nevertheless, it was great to watch the moody ocean as the large ocean swells in the near distance randomly peaked, peeled and slammed down on the reefs fringing the shore. The waves on this exposed shore looked a solid double or more overhead. Technically you could call some of them surfable. If they were located back home some would be named surf spots and be surfed regularly. But in a solid swell they were ugly and awe inspiring rather than genuine surf options.

A huge peak would steam across in the distance with all

of us mentally surfing it only to see it shut down horribly on some shallow lump of coral. Most of all there were no channels – nowhere to run to or to allow you back out through the break after a wave. At one point my imagination put me in a horrible spot as a huge set steamed in over my pictured flick off point. A shiver went down my spine and I looked quickly around and fixed my eyes on the surrounding safety and comforts of the boat to dispel the imagery of impending doom.

In the Mentawais, as with huge stretches of the coral lined coasts across the tropics, the only quality surf spots are where a very defined gap in the reef exists and the even tapering of the coral shelf is so straight and clean that it could shape the waves into peeling lines. Mostly coral reefs consist of countless miles of jagged rock walls that are too straight or which shelve upwards too rapidly and produced bone-crunching closeouts. Occasionally, a curve in the coast combined with a gap or even slope in the reef gives the endless ocean swells a respite from being formless walls and a surf spot is created. In the Mentawais these set ups were more common than almost anywhere else.

Lance's Lefts – our destination - is just such a spot. The exposed south western tip of the island's coastline takes a sharp curve around into a long half moon bay lined by coconut palms and a shimmering white beach. As the long ocean swells from as far away as Africa bend into the bay the peel rate slows from that of a speeding train to that of a loping tiger. The rotating swells lose a little bit of size and intensity in the process. The bend also seems to settle them into cleaner lines. The mechanics of the break begin miles away from the take off zone and culminate in a final 300 metre stretch of reef before the beach, which produces a fantastic long left that is a mix of power and grace.

Of course, on this day, we were not greeted by perfection. The wind was straight onshore and chop was ruining the 4-5ft waves. Skelts was rightly fuming. I kept my mouth shut and hoped for something to be salvaged from the bad move.

The wind seemed to have some north west to it and was coming from roughly in the direction of a fun right-hander called Bintangs across the bay. To me it looked almost offshore and sheltered over there. There was plenty of swell as proven by the bombie thundering away in the middle of the bay. We went over for a look. Bintangs is a hard wave to check properly unless you are close. You almost have to be in the line-up to really see it well.

As with HTs, it benefits from a sharp swing of the swell around an outer reef hooking it into a concentrated peak that sucks below sea level in a way much in common with your typical Australian reef break. It is shallow but somehow friendlier by reputation and experience than HTs.

Somewhat confused waves were breaking on the reef with spray blowing off their backs – a sure sign that the waves were curving around the reef far enough to let the wind become virtually off the shore – meaning clean faces. My spirits lifted as I looked forward to a fun afternoon surfing one of my favourite waves in the

Mentawais. To my eyes, it seemed at least head high and if the amount of swell hitting the bombie nearby was any indication, it might even be bigger. Bintangs was one of those waves that sucked out below sea level creating a clean face even in choppy conditions. I thought it was obvious that this was the spot for the afternoon surf and stood leaning on the rail sizing up the options waiting for the anchor to be dropped so I could grab my board and hit the water.

No-one else seemed interested though. It looked too messy from the back view of the waves. Next thing I knew it was my turn to wonder what the hell was going on as the boat veered back to Lances Lefts. The Skipper had made his only bad call of the trip. It was a classic case of where a surf spot looked a bit ugly but the quality of the reef set up would be enough to overcome the flawed conditions. We never got close enough for anyone else to share my view.

On deck Dr Paul had quickly assessed the afternoon's surf options and resumed reading his Kindle. He was patiently biding his time for the right conditions to present themselves whereupon he could emerge as a wave catching demon on his favourite inside take-off spot. He knew his fun zone very well and was content to enjoy a cruising holiday interspersed with surf whenever the waves were in the fun category.

Paul also kept eyeing off a new piece of safety equipment on the Addiction, an orange contraption called a spinal board, with a loving and satisfied gaze. Paul was not a doctor but his first aid skills had been honed in the surf lifesaving movement back home in Australia. He always travelled with an extensive medical kit and was treated by one and all as Dr Paul.

On his last trip he had been forced to care for an over-zealous surf guide from a nearby boat who had insisted on showing his guests just how to take off behind the peak at one of the world's best lefts - Macaronis - on wave after wave. He back-doored the shallowest section of the reef each time. I am sure his guest got the point and would have been happy to have him stop the lesson and let them have a few more waves to catch. Fate intervened and they got their wish when he took another shallow peak and went over the falls onto the reef below.

The coral scalped him leaving a flap of a flesh and blood toupee hanging over his face. Being the fastest boat The Addiction had to do its duty and overnight him back across the Sumatran Strait to Padang. Paul dealt with both the bloody wound and the possibility of spinal injury complications as best he could. After this he had no trouble talking the Skipper into buying a spinal board for the boat and was pleased to see it freshly purchased there for all to see.

Meanwhile, back in the top cabin, after a brief stir to roll over, Hoover, the hard working cray fisherman and cattle farmer, savoured the opportunity to be away from the endless demands of work and slept on.

Dean emerged from his cabin and joined a slightly flat, unenthused and, in a couple of cases, guilty bunch of wave warriors sweltering under the glare of the tropical sun and a still steaming and self-righteous Skelts. We hit the surf.

The chop made paddling out to the waves hard and then catching them even harder. Occasionally, the chop would help push you into a wave but mostly they seemed to actively resist being caught. I snagged three medium sized waves in an hour long session. They looked lame in the photos that night but amazed me with the speed I was travelling and the distance I covered. The 6'6" McCoy felt great. Somehow, I dodged all the on-the-head wide sets and did not wipe-out or have to dive once. I headed in after my third wave quitting while I was ahead. Others were not so lucky.

Dean, as usual, went way inside us all looking for the long, fast, bigger ones. But his slow take-offs combined with the chop and sections soon gave him a quick trip across the whole reef, including the inside shallow stretch that the lies in wait before the lagoon near the beach. He received a lift out in the rubber ducky to join us in the take off zone only to repeat this dangerous and exhausting cycle two more times during the surf. The waves were a mix of rolling shoulders and then big wide sets – often bumpy and fat but with some heavy sections that could really smash you about.

Taff was swept inside after one wipe-out and ended up in knee deep water with a five foot wall of water sucking up and smashing down on him. All he could do was leap up onto it and stick his board below him as some sort of protection and hope for the best. Luckily he was blasted across the reef into deep water near the beach board and body unscratched. He paddled out very sober and wary after what he called one of his most scary reef encounters ever.

Overall, the surf was short but not sweet for most of us. I was, however, pretty happy after three good waves and no reef trouble. Dean persisted longest sitting too far inside punching through wave after wave in pursuit of what he told us later was the cleaner fourth wave of the set. We all watched him out there alone from the comfort of the boat. The waves all looked like an onshore beach break with the added complication of a coral bottom. On his final trip over the falls he wrenched his shoulder and was left wondering about how he would even paddle the next day.

Back on board, on the mention of the word injury by Dean, Paul perked up and glanced across at the spinal board lying untested nearby. Unfortunately though there appeared to be nothing neck or back related going on so with a sigh of disappointment her picked up his Kindle and went back to reading – his spinal expertise unappreciated.

Hoover, meanwhile, was still on his bunk, sound asleep reveling in every minute of his 2012 Mentawai trip.

We headed off with ice cold Bintangs in hand to our overnight mooring. Hoover finally emerged from his lair to begin catching up on the many hours smoking time he had missed whilst asleep. Coops revealed a major talent and let fly with some loud farts for all to enjoy right in the middle of conversations. Dean held the floor with more well worn but entertaining tales of past trips and youthful misadventures back in his home state before he left for the big city.

On reflection, the day felt like a weird mix of perfection, fear, tension, chop and slop. I was left with the realisation that the new friends in the amalgam of tour members drawn together by Dean could surf and were going to get their share of waves. Taff, Dean and I had the luxury on the last trip of having the pick of the waves on many days due to the prevalence of bad hips, crook backs, cracked vertebrae, injured Achilles tendons, coral aversion and cracking DVDs among the "old mates" who ventured on the "reunion" trip.

I had learned two important lessons– don't make big calls on which spot to surf without a lot of thought and should have learned another – look inside when taking off so you don't drop in on "le hyper-musclé French monsieur".

That night Dean presented the Mentawai Misfits T shirt (awarded and inscribed each day for noteworthy events or achievements) to the most outstanding tour member of Day 1. His choice was a man was famous as a magnet for trouble when travelling and in airports;   a man as strong as an ox but with hips of broken glass and a backbone worn by heavy lifting; a man who valued a cigarette above catching a flight on time for the holiday of a lifetime. But his crowning achievement on this day was to have travelled halfway around the world to the remotest islands of Sumatra to spend the first sunny day of tropical perfection sleeping on a narrow little bunk bed, snoring to his heart's content. Hoover we all agreed had his priorities right and knew how to seize the day!

Of course we all knew that Hoover was actually quite paddle fit on this trip and was patient. He would pick his days to emerge and do his thing – speed runs across the face on a new superfast board (currently somewhere in Padang). These rides were made even more memorable by being preceded by some of the most difficult, bad-hip-induced one-legged take-offs ever witnessed in the Mentawais. Hoover through necessity would get one leg up and then use his hands to lift the other into position, all the while heading down the face of the wave – a stunt probably never seen in the Mentawais before.

**Hoover with Karangniki palms in the backdrop**

## 2. MENTAWAIN FEAST

**Afternoon Bintangs - could it be more inviting?**

In the mornings, on The Addiction, a pattern emerged among the tour members. There were the very early risers, the early risers, the just on timers and the late risers. Tim was the earliest riser generally but never seemed to eat breakfast and just sat up on deck smoking and watching the ocean. Perhaps his lungs had evolved ways of extracting nutrients from smoke. Doug would usually join me for breakfast upon hearing the clink of the bowls but one day surprised me by mentioning that this was his second breakfast - his first being at about 4am. This meant by mid-morning he often had three breakfasts! I never asked about the logic of the 4 am breakfast and thought it was probably part of his strategy to ensure that there was no possible way that Charlie could hit the water before him.

Dean was mostly an early riser. Sometimes he was up and about around 4 am probably doing emails to keep his staff back home on their toes. Taff and Skelts just seemed to appear as we reached whatever surf spot we were going to - never early but never late. Charlie, ever vigilant, would just appear like clockwork about the time Doug poured milk on his bowl of Cornflakes.

I can't remember Coops at breakfast at all throughout the tour but on most days he would just be there ready to hit the water only a few minutes behind the rest of us.

Coops is the world's happiest retiree, surfing on the Sunshine Coast at his leisure. I had learned the night before, chatting in our cabin, that he began surfing in the sixties and had experienced that dreamlike era of Queensland in the late sixties and early seventies first hand. He told me of being out at Noosa with just a few guys at T-Trees, no crowds and no cares except timing the arrival of the next swell. Coops had actually lived my surf fantasies fuelled as a young surfer, by the surfing magazines that I read endlessly cover to cover. Whilst he was up there steaming across long running tropical point break perfection, I was down in the deep south shivering as I rode short, cold Tasmanian beach breaks, mostly pretending I was living the dream. I was envious and intrigued as I listened to his stories each evening.

Coops eventually became responsible and drifted somewhat from surfing having a successful career in property and project management. But his roots in the sixties had brought him back to the surf and he was again a frothing grommet at 61! These roots also had drawn him to alternative health approaches.

Cabin mate Hoover, interestingly, could not have had more contrasting philosophies on health than Coops. Coops trusted in Meridian Lines and had possibly even studied under Sting himself how to sustain tantric sex sessions for eight hours of pleasure. Mark put his faith in powerful triple strength horse liniment. Each evening, before bed, he would ladle huge gobs of white cream over his aching back and hips, making the eyes of his cabin mates burn and water with its fumes. He offered some to us but warned us not to get the stuff anywhere near eyes or any other sensitive areas as it would "sting like crap".

I wondered at the time about the potential for liniment related accidents between the sheets of the marital bed back home on Hoover's farm due to this nightly procedure and the broad spread of the cream across his body. No wonder his wife looked so pleased at the airport to pack him off to the Mentawais for a few weeks.

* * *

It was not long after I finished my breakfast when The Addiction reached the bay leading to Lance's Lefts. We passed over some solid groundswells on the trip over. Each powerful line that swept under the boat raised our hopes for the day's surfing ahead. The lack of wind in the bay and anywhere out to sea was magic to see. The sea was oily smooth to the far horizon.

The Addiction moved fast. We sped across the last stretch, past the bombora breaking top to bottom in the middle of the bay, and finally swung into the anchorage spot. The crowd on deck all could see that it was on ... and empty!

Lance's Lefts was glassy, well overhead and peeling evenly for 150 metres or more. I sped up my simple preparations to hit the water. On with the bathers, then the lycra shorts to protect me from rash, then the boardshorts, next the rash vest, followed by the second padded rash vest (home-made pads to protect the soft skin over my ribs that was used to a wetsuit for protection) with the first vest to stop rash from the second vest. Next was sunscreen, then the hat, followed by some blue tack in the ears to keep water out, reef booties and finally a band aid on the back of my heel to stop chafing from one bootie. "Ahhhh" I thought, "the freedom of surfing in the tropics".

I hopped in the tender with Doug and Charlie for the first run out to the peak. Before long Dean, Skelts, Taff and Coops were out there too. My first wave was a set with a long drop and a huge wall stretching across the bay. I took it easy, sweeping up and down in long turns at eye-watering speed and flicked off amazed at the distance I had covered.

That remained a huge impression from every wave - speed. The photos that night never really captured this or the length of the wave. It was fast but also mostly easy to make. There were pauses in its roll along the reef allowing for cutbacks and other turns.

The session turned out to be a classic. It wasn't quite a total "wave fest" as there were long waits between sets and typically there were only two to four waves per set to be shared around. Over the morning I caught about eight big, solid waves and progressively pushed my turns harder as the session wore on. The McCoy just flew and accelerated in cutbacks but with that sense of control you want in bigger waves. A couple of photos that night managed to capture a hint of that cutback speed.

I sat just to the edge of the shallow inside take off along with Doug, Charlie, Taff and Skelts. Coops was in a bit picking off the medium sized ones partly so he could tell his wife back home that he did not take any risks. As the photos showed that night, Coops caught a lot of waves in there by the shallowest section of the reef and so took no risks at all! I was enjoying the big take-offs and being able to escape from, or sometimes catch, any wide sets that came through. Coops must have dodged or copped on the head a lot of serious sets that day sitting in there as I only just punched through the lip of some monster blue walls. My approach on this trip was mostly to sit outside to get better, larger waves and to be far away from the shallow inside reefs. Big was safer.

Dean, of course, went 15 metres inside to sit on the shallow spot where the take-offs were much steeper and faster and consequences a lot more serious. Obviously, this was the perfect spot for someone with a sore shoulder and a notoriously slow take-off.

The rest of us had a box seat view of Dean's technique: paddle for a heavy wave, stop paddling about 2 strokes too early, slowly haul his bulk to his feet to stand up and start the drop. The wave by this time had curled over forcing Dean to drop with the broken lip, or in the falling white water in a very difficult situation. The drama was not over yet. Once Dean hit the bottom he had to bottom turn. Usually this was not a clean turn on an open face but through and around the exploding white water to finally reach the wave face. By this time he was either wiped out, in major trouble or right in the pocket for a potential tube.

Dean has a somewhat famous youtube video of him getting caught inside at Lance's lefts by a 10 footer with Charlie cackling from the safety of the tender. What is not known is that he ended up almost drowning with his legrope caught on some coral way down deep. He had a two wave hold down (a very serious event in surfing) and only survived because his legrope broke. He ended up washed in over the reef totally naked as the wipeout had blasted his boardshorts off. Despit this experience Dean always paddled right back to that same inside spot every time he surfed Lance's Lefts.

Dean got the best tubes of the trip - mainly in later sessions at Thunders - so there was method in his madness. It was very gutsy to do that continually all trip long at every spot. Dean sat in harm's way not just occasionally like the rest of us but day in and day out.

Early in this surf his strike rate was pretty low making it amusing and a little frustrating to watch. The

temptation to take off in front of him when you knew
he had blown it was high but drop-ins of any type were
the number one sin on these trips so we all resisted. By
the end of the trip his wipe-out frequency reduced and
the radical deep positions on hollow waves become
something to see.

* * *

Dean was at first glance an unlikely looking veteran of
six of these trips. He looked like a guy more at home on
the couch or motoring around in a golf cart on a lazy
beer soaked corporate golf day than charging Mentawai
barrels. A highlight of the trip was always when he
paddled into the occasional crowded line up of a shallow
reef break populated with a mix of young, fit, tanned
and nimble surfers hugging the inside take off spot. He
would paddle leisurely along perched up high on his big
mini mal surfboard by his barrel chest and a similarly
proportioned gut looking like the wrong guy in the right
place. As surfers do, they would, at a glance, sum up his
place in the pecking order and as a competitor for
precious waves. My guess was the quick summation was
usually "no competition" or "shoulder hopper" or even
"dangerous obstacle". But then to their surprise, Dean
would steadily keep paddling past the safe take off zone
into the inside of the hot young rippers, sit up and start
chatting away. Then, when a set came, he would
proceed to paddle straight into the next heavy peak from
way inside.

If it was day one or two, what followed was often both
horrific and greatly entertaining for all. His friends had

seen it all before but still found it perversely gripping as we watched from 20 metres away at the safer and more logical take-off spot. It was like watching an overweight but artful bull fighter, a few steps slower than his peak, facing a nimble aggressive young bull. The danger was real, the coral was sharp, the inside zone was meant for young fit surfers with months of recent Indonesian surf under the belt – not a middle aged corporate executive.

For the young rippers looking on I am sure it was just as fascinating and perplexing as they wondered silently "what the hell is that big guy doing?" By day three he would be making most of his waves. Oddly, his slowness would almost serve as a purposeful stalling technique, placing his thick set frame deep in the tube. Further down the line, with speed to burn, he would slash a huge cutback throwing spray further and thicker than any professional surfer could manage with their whip thin 70 kg frames.

A week later, at a heavy spot called Thunders, one of our tour members overheard a young guy from another charter boat say to a friend as he paddled out after witnessing Dean fly by after coming from deep inside, "I love watching that big guy surf". Somehow the unlikely juxtaposition of bulk, power and grace under pressure made some of his moves more impressive than even the predictable acrobatics of professional surfers.

* * *

Lance's Lefts gave me a chance to see the Sydney boys in action at the take off and on the long paddles back out. First impressions were of older confident, solid surfers, comfortable in big waves and dealing with coral reefs. As sets arrived, they swung around and went with no fuss, drama or hesitation. One thing I noticed was they knew how to stake their claim on a wave through positioning. There was no aggressive paddle to the inside. Rather, they made sure they were in the spot or paddling for the spot with their body language doing the talking saying very clearly; "this is mine", something that must be essential in crowded Sydney surf. But there were other subtle differences in approach. Skelts to me was like Taff and I in where he sat and how he paddled for waves. You knew exactly what he was doing and when he was going.

Doug took longer to read. He specialised in the late, almost no paddle take off. Doug would sit watching the wave approach past the point I would have had my head down and be paddling. This left you guessing a bit as it was easy to assume he did not really want it. I was often tempted to swing round and take the wave. I soon learned that he would almost always take it unless, being someone big on taking turns in the water, he felt that it was somebody else's turn. I couldn't always work out which of these options he was planning. Sometimes Doug would leave his paddle too late and miss the wave but he had remarkable paddling ability for someone who was not obviously muscle bound.

Charlie was something quite different altogether in technique and wave catching approach. I finally got to see first-hand the famous pig dog take-off I had heard so much about. He was renowned for taking off on his backhand in a slight crouch, sideways, ready for a tube.

It was almost a classic backhand tube stance but with a kooky variation – feet too close together – that made it look unstable. But it worked. Charlie could, and would, take off in all sorts of ridiculous positions under the lip and in the white water of grinding barrels and virtually always make it. I swung around many times expecting him pull back on an overly late take-off on heavy grinding lefts. Eventually I gave up, as with almost no exception, go he would, standing up in a crouch initially and then upright once he was off and running. He surfed well but you almost willed him to step that back foot onto the sweet spot and get the full benefit of it to drive his turns. In some distant past he had picked up a particular habit and was sticking to it no matter what.

Charlie shone by making some difficult take-offs of the trip on Day 2, in the maw of some throaty beasts that would have amazed even the most jaded Indonesian surfer..

\* \* \*

After a few hours empty bellies and the midday sun drove the guys back to the comfort of the boat. I was left alone in long perfect lefts. It had become very inconsistent though and I would almost snooze off between sets in the midday heat. Still, every 150 metre well-overhead wave is an event worth waiting for. It was very peaceful between waves sitting out in the water admiring the brilliant white sweep of the distant beach and green hues of coconut palms, contrasting with the blue of the ocean. The water was lukewarm, enough for total comfort, but not so warm that it was not a refreshing salve when it washed over my sun-cooked back. In between waves I would put my sun hat on, which I soaked in water, and sit in the pleasant shade of its evaporating coolness. With proper sun protection, the water was the best place to be in the midday heat. All I needed was an ice cold drink and perhaps a pillow to rest my head (the waits for sets were getting longer).

Up to that point, I had not wiped out all day. I had also just managed to scrape over the top of all the big set waves and so had not had to fully duck dive a set. Big waves, with no rough and tumble – it seemed too good to be true. The ocean soon fixed that.

A really big set came through. Perhaps the biggest I had seen all day. I woke myself out of my tropical stupor and paddled wide as fast as I could. I really wanted to catch it. Angling around, I stroked hard and for a moment looked over the ledge and thought for a second that I was into it. I was pushed up vertically as the wave rose to full height but was stuck up there on the back of the wave as it curled beneath me. For a moment I was suspended at that tipping point where I might just be able to slip out backwards and escape its clutches. Then, suddenly, I broke through the curtain of the lip that had formed below me and was in free fall lying sideways inside the tube half curled into a ball. I looked down and had time to think that it sure looked like I was falling a long way and braced myself for the impact. The resulting thrashing was fairly major making up for all the wipeouts I had dodged all day. I was finally let up keen for some air way in near the inside section. It had dragged me a good 50 metres underwater. Fortunately the long distance swell from a storm somewhere off Africa had thrown up a one wave set. Even so, another medium sized wave loomed towards me and the shallow reef was just a stone's throw shoreward. I grabbed my board and paddled hard for the shoulder and just made it over into the channel cleanly. If a big set had followed I would have most likely been dragged over the shallow inside section suffering who know what? It was one of my most memorable wipe outs ever and oddly became a highlight of the day.

Eventually, after savouring the empty line up for another hour or so, picking off some more long fast walls, I headed in for some food when a few guys from the land camp paddled out. I had been in the water from dawn to well after lunch. The Addiction was full of all the tour members talking of waves ridden, eating food and checking out the photos Geni had taken. I stuffed some food down quickly, drank a few glasses of water and lay down for 10 minutes to close sore eyes. With quality waves around I could not settle into sleep or a book and so was soon on deck again getting ready to duck out again while things were quiet. Taff was also getting his gear on. Quietly he mentioned to me "I am thinking of going to Bintangs". "I'm in" I said immediately.

Bintangs was the perfect option for an afternoon of low-stress fun when arms were tired. It was a hotdog wave with a short paddle and a barrel take-off. Coops decided to come along in the dingy to check it out with us. On the trip over the outside Bombie was just exploding top to bottom – a spectacular sight close up.

I was totally confident that Bintangs would be really good. We pulled up, I looked for about 10 seconds and thought "why wait" and jumped over and started paddling hard for the peak. Taff followed trusting my judgment. Coops, was more skeptical and watched for a while. As I paddled not much was happening on the peak and I could see why Coops was hesitating. Taff and I reached the line-up and waited. Coops left on the dingy before the first real set arrived to go back to Lance's Lefts.

Then a set came and we scrambled for the shoulder as the magical aqua blue below-sea-level-suck-out occurred so reminiscent of Eaglehawk Reef back in Tasmania. We missed the first few waves but just looked at each other knowing it was on. What followed was a very special surf. We caught so many waves and talked of how amazing it was to have only two of us out in perfect surf. The tubes on the take-off were elusive as you would tend to outrun them but the shoulder invited big cutbacks and sometimes a hollow inside section popped up. It was quite shallow inside but this never worried me as by then you were up and riding and in control of when to flick off and when to keep running through the sections.

Surf breaks give out a sort of vibe and Bintangs seemed a friendly sort. It was a quick paddle to the shoulder if a set swung wide and the white water lost its brute force rapidly which helped keep you out of trouble. Also it felt like an Australian reef break in many ways due to the way the peak sucked out. It had a familiar feel. Strangely, some wipeouts on the peak seemed as shallow as HTs but my mind convinced me I was much safer and I tumbled away a foot above the coral unconcerned whereas, in the same situation, given the aura of HTs, I would have been expecting doom.

During this surf, with so many waves to let go, ride or waste you could think "what will I do next, try for a tube maybe, do an off the top perhaps?". To me, surfing in this situation is the peak experience of the whole sport. My mind was at peace. An empty reef wave means that the distractions of beachbreaks and more fickle and crowded locations, such as competing for waves, worries that a crowd might appear or concerns that tide or wind cold ruin the surf were absent. It was perfect and it was going to stay that way – a rare event back home.

Taff was surfing really well doing some great cutbacks and pocket rides hoping for a tube. He is one of those rare surfers whose surfing has improved a lot since his early 20s – mostly in the last 10 years. Back in the 1970s I had a 3-4 year head start on him by getting seriously into surfing from 13 onwards. He started later and then caught up quickly but remained a bit stiff and slow in his turns – too much muscle at times. Once his son got interested in surfing he got right back into it during his 40s and these days surfs more than me. Being a PE teacher and all-round sportsman into martial arts he had worked on his surfing technique rather than just staying static as is common for virtually all surfers past about 25 years of age. His style has improved a lot as had quite a few of his moves - forehand and backhand cutbacks in particular - both of which are technically very good but also often pretty radical. The Tae Kwon Do he did regularly had clearly made him far more flexible and attuned him to doing body and arm movements in technically correct ways to the point that even how he held his hands during a turn seemed artful and controlled.

Taff and Coops were certainly polar opposites when it came to arms control when surfing. Coops' arm movements were quite wild and unpredictable. He was the free form innovator of "The Pizza Delivery", The "Back Scratch Cutback", and "The Balinese Shadow Puppet Off the Lip". Taff was the Black Belt technician.

My own surfing had the benefit of the early start at 13, a brother with a driving license and shack at a local surf beach. I surfed a lot. The factors for fast progression were not that favourable though. Classic long waves are not common in Tasmania. Sadly, while multiple world class spots exist not that far from where I live, most are hidden behind peninsulas, islands and tucked away from the brunt of swell and only work occasionally, and then, often for a day or even just a morning. Mostly I grew up surfing very average beach breaks and, in the middle 1970s, boards had gone long and thin inspired by the surf media's focus on Hawaii. I was riding a 7 foot single fin pin tail in 3 foot beach breaks for years! The only thing this board did well was off the lips and re-entries – pivot off the bottom and bang off the lip. Good cut backs were almost impossible until the waves were solid.

The off-the-lip became my specialty and I viewed every

section as a chance to do one. I would get up vertical with just the tail and fin in the water and 7 foot of board sticking up in sky and make most of them. They felt great to do and were even for their time quite a radical move but I was a bit one dimensional as a surfer.

It was not until twin fins came along that my surfing became more rounded. The overnight transition from my 7 foot pintail to a 6' 2" Mark Richards twin fin was one of the most exciting times in my surfing history. Suddenly, I could do cutbacks at will in small waves. On my first surf on my new twin fin, I went out in waist high beach breaks and jammed them over and over in gutless waves. I have nostalgia for the waves back in the early 1970s but not for the boards. Overall, I became a pretty good surfer with some good moves, but never one who could rip any wave, anytime. As with most surfers, the better the waves, the better I surfed.

By my early twenties, after a few years on three finned thrusters, I reached a plateau and for the next 30 years I surfed pretty much the same with surf quality and fitness being the main factors influencing performance. In the middle of winter if I was unfit and stiff with cold I was usually pretty average. Now, in the warmth of the tropics and quality waves, the years fell away and I felt 21 again.

* * *

After a while Tim came over for his first surf of the trip. It was not easy for Tim watching the waves at HTs and Lance's from the boat rather than riding them himself.

However, with almost no peripheral vision or depth perception it was a sensible decision to wait. Most people with his eyesight would be would be on the couch at home - not sitting off a shallow reef in Indonesia trying to catch waves! So it was Taff, Tim and I surfing together - just like old times.

In between waves, Taff and I tried to help Tim pick some peaks to go for. The medium sized ones had pretty straightforward take-offs so we told him to paddle in near the peak to catch these. Obediently he would paddle in and wait. Then a set would come and clobber him on the head. Next he would move towards the shoulder and sit too wide just missing the next few good ones. Again, we would then convince him to edge in closer and cruelly, sure enough, a big set would suck out into an aqua blue bowl out the back and steam through to clean him up. Back and forth he went getting hammered over and over. In the end we just shut up and hoped things would turn around somehow.

His description of his vision was that it was like looking down a narrow tube with no peripheral vision at all. He had been unaware of the problem until a routine medical test a few years before when he got the shock of his life hearing that he was actually legally blind. He went in with a headache and left without a driving license and his world turned upside down. Apparently his brain had learned to fill in the gaps in his vision with whatever made sense to it. This meant that when driving a car, virtually everything outside what was straight in front of him was not even real. His brain made up trees, curbs and houses where none existed! Somehow he had unknowingly compensated and survived on the roads. Since then his vision had slowly become worse. His depth perception was very poor making take-offs difficult. Oddly, in a narrow tunnel straight ahead he could see quite well, so once up and riding could still enjoy a wave.

Finally, after a while, I spotted a medium sized one that was heading straight for Tim. Taff and I called to him "Go!" He swung around on pure trust, probably with no idea what the wave he was trying to catch looked like, and paddled. Taff and I looked on willing him into it. We were stoked to see him perfectly positioned on the edge of the peak pick up speed and get to his feet and head off on the wave. He rode it right through to the inside section and was back on the path to becoming Indo Man again. Taff and I were as stoked as Tim.

After 3 hours of surfing Bintangs I was a little tired but still took some convincing to go back for a late lunch – it was too much fun to waste time eating. I only did so when I knew that Taff planned to come straight back.

On the second surf there - our third session for the day - Tim, Hoover and Paul joined us. The rest of the guys surfed Lances Lefts and got plenty of good waves.

Hoover arrived on a huge borrowed longboard with his Captain Cook sun hat on and proceeded to paddle the "Endeavour" way out to sea, well out from the peak, where he sat for a long while in deep water. We were busy inside catching waves. Eventually Captain Hoover stirred into action. He pulled up anchor and started to

tack back and forth scanning the coast with his
telescope, charting the hazards, shoals and reefs in the
wax on his board. Periodically he would throw out the
sounding line and pull up the wax plug and study it to
assess depth and bottom substrate. Finally, he decided it
was time for action and after one last sighting with his
sextant he pointed his board to shore and was soon at
top speed.

Taff yelled out "Look out" and we both scrambled for
safety as Hoover picked up speed towards us. Spray was
flying from powerful arms and a wake developed as he
paddled flat out for a wave he had spotted from way
outside. It was classic Hoover - sit around doing
nothing and then suddenly wake up and pick on some
unsuspecting wave transforming from sleepy bear to
paddling machine. He would absolutely commit to
catching his wave often from way too far out and chase
the damn thing down with grim determination scattering
and intimidating anyone else in his way.

If Hoover went - forget it - getting out of his way was
the only sensible option. On another day at
Burgerworld I saw this strategy work to perfection in a
moderate crowd from the other boats. A couple of
pretty good surfers had eyed off a wave and just totally
pulled back as he steamed towards them. They knew he
was going no matter what and left him well alone. Back
at Bintangs, Captain Hoover somehow caught that
uncatchable wave and rode it all the way for a great start
to his first surf on the trip.

Paul in the meantime had worked out just where to sit

to do his specialty - pick the medium and wide ones whilst being well placed to dodge the bigger sets. Cautious at first, soon he was catching wave after wave and riding them with panache and good functional turns through to the inside. Throughout the trip Paul patiently waited out the bigger, meaner days and then more than made up for it by feasting once the conditions met his simple criteria – fun waves.

On The Addiction that night everyone was stoked and surfed out. Best of all, we were alone at the mooring, so no other charter boats seemed interested in Lance's Lefts. With the swell holding and not much wind, it looked like the next day would be a repeat of this one. We all sat around the ice chest cold beer or coke in hand savouring a great day. I cast my eye around the fellow drinkers. There was Dean holding court telling tales about girls, vodka and washing machines at his party house a long time ago. Taff was standing strategically by the rails where the evening sun hit his six-pack at the perfect angle to maximise the light and shadow definition. Coops was looking serene and mystical wearing his sarong. Every now and then Coops undertook a yoga-inspired Tantric Evacuation of Unclean Air procedure and the faint smell of spices, incense and last night's curry wafted over the appreciative group.

That night I had no idea who would win the T-shirt. I was just surfed out after one of the most full on days of surfing I had ever had. Coops emerged as the winner for the amazing achievement of being on the trip after a triple bypass only three months before and going straight out into solid waves. The photos revealed Coops as a wave catching machine. Time after time there he was, a brightly coloured tropical fish (the brightest board and rash vest combination ever seen in the Mentawais), ripping on perfect solid lefts. At 61, when so many surfers are content to trim along small waves at Greenmount or Noosa, there was Coops taking on the heavy waves of the Mentawais – a very impressive physical and mental effort.

Coops also had displayed to his new tour friends his almost inimitable body English with those unique, twisting arm movements dazzling us as he zipped up and down the waves when surfing. Former four time world champion, Mark Richard, strange arm positioning had labeled him The Wounded Seagull in his prime. Coops made Mark's style look boringly conventional and he had deservedly earned his moniker "The Pizza Delivery Man". A label any surfer would wear with pride.

**Coops – Pizza Man delivering the goods at Thunders**

Clive M. Woodward

## 3. SECOND HELPINGS

**The amazing view as we made ready to paddle out**

The next morning dawned with the usual balmy, tropical warmth of the equatorial latitudes. There was barely a cloud in the sky. The common huge cumulus cloud billows of the tropics sat out on the horizon. Beyond the shelter of the bay, the ocean stretched to the horizon with the glassy patterns of a windless ocean broken here and there by occasional textured patches darkened by ruffles of wind. Tim and I sat quietly and watched the dawn break turning the water's tones from black to golden hues and eventually the deep blue of the tropics.

I loved looking out across the ocean late at night and early in the morning when it was quiet and no one much was around to break the mood. At night the sky was lit up by stars and sometimes distant lightning flashes. The stars seemed twice as bright and ten times as many as back home in suburbia. On the open ocean horizon

there would always be the bright glow of Indonesian
fishing boats which had massive lights strung up to
attract in fish. These were periodically scooped up in
huge dragon fly wing shaped nets. In the deep tropical
night they glowed like spooky alien space craft.
Between them was a deep blackness and the lonely
undulating Indian Ocean stretching all the way to Africa.

In the dark of night, if you directed your gaze away from
any lights it became easy to conjure up the visions and
sensations of a tropical days long past.  I could become
a South Sea Islander hidden in the splendid isolation of
the tropics, contemplating the sense of predictability and
peace of the next day's fishing on my coral fringed
lagoon.  I'd be an early British explorer, sitting on my
boat off a dark and foreboding jungle-covered island,
wondering what reception the natives would provide on
landfall the next morning.  I could be Thor Heyerdahl
on my balsa wood raft drifting with the current under
the starlit heavens.

The mornings, meanwhile, were not for imaginings.
Instead, they were a brief, peaceful pause in my day
before plunging again into whatever surf was available
and commencing my hunt for crystalline cylinders.
There would be a sunrise to watch, wind to note and
hints of swell to muse over.

Our moorings were peaceful spots where we could only
feel the vaguest roll of swell.  We stayed in sheltered
bays well off the coast away from mosquitoes and
potential tsunami exposure.  The Skippers of charter
boats were playing it very safe these days after a major

tsunami took out a boat – The Midas – which had been moored in the bay at the famed surf break. Macaronis.

Fortunately, I was not on the boat at the time but had actually travelled on it only few months before it was smashed by the huge tsunami that hit the Mentawais in 2010. The Midas was partly swamped and caught fire and burned to the water line. The comfortable cabin I had once slept in each night downstairs was the scene of a dramatic escape.

Macaronis has a sheltered inner bay that was once a popular overnight mooring spot for boat charters. I had spent two night in there on the Midas rocking away in the residual swell unaware of the risk on my first trip to the Mentawais. On the night of the Tsunami, Rick, the Skipper, and most of the surfers on board were on the upper deck enjoying an evening drink when they heard a load roar from out to sea. Rick knew instinctively that it was something very much at odds with any normal sound of the surf. He raced to start the boat, up anchor and head out to sea. Before he could get The Midas away, however, the wave was upon them and a huge wall of water swept a nearby boat into The Midas with a sickening crunch. A gas bottle exploded and the boat caught fire.

Under an hour before, well off the coast, tectonic pressures that had built for years finally broke the sea floor on a fault line and a major uplift of the sea floor occurred which displaced a huge volume of water. This sent out a pulse of energy in the form of a series of tsunamis aimed directly at the southern Mentawai

Islands. The sequences of waves moved fast and low in deep water but built dramatically in size upon reaching the coast. For The Midas crew and surfers, being on the water meant that the warning sign of the earthquake was not noticed and so they all sat oblivious as the powerful waves marched towards them. The wide-mouthed bay that so effectively groomed swells to create the famed surf break at Macaronis, became a funnel, concentrating and building the waves to greater heights until deep in the bay they were broken walls of water with immense power.

Once the boat was hit and on fire, Rick told everyone to dive overboard and they were soon being swept off in the dark by successive huge waves into the mangroves and jungle that lined the coast.

Tsunami waves are not like normal waves at all. They have behind them a thick, deep energy that does not let up after they break. Broken waves surge forward with the weight of the ocean behind them. They can wash boats far inland, smash trees like trigs and hold human victims pinned against obstacles underwater unable to move.

The surfers being swept away were experienced in the water and stayed calm. Some of the crew were poor swimmers. In the pitch dark they had to fight the successive waves that threatened to entangle them under water in the mass of mangrove roots. Some surfers had been in the downstairs cabin. Two managed to come up the stairs and leap through the flames and overboard. Two others did not make it out and were stuck in their cabin.

Once in the jungle, the bedraggled, bruised and battered surfers and crew clung to trees to stop from being swept deeper into the mangroves and to stay above water. They slowly re-grouped, calling to each other to move to a central place. Rick went through the frightening process of doing a roll call and to his relief, all the crew and surfers had somehow survived. Apparently the two stuck below deck had squeezed out of the small port holes in the downstairs cabin.

This dramatic event brought home the vulnerability of certain mooring spots and now all the charter boats headed deep into protected lee shores each evening as a precaution. It also sent shock waves around the world to former Midas passengers who, like me, could all too vividly imagine the disaster and frightening night time trip into the jungle in the grip of an unseen Tsunami. We were also saddened by the ruin and loss of life it caused to many local villages near the coast. Surfaid raised money from surfers across the world specifically to help these often forgotten isolated islands.

The plate tectonics that cause tsunamis impact the Mentawais surf in other ways. They actually change the seafloor through violent uplifts and subsidence making the surfing reefs deeper or shallower. The 2010 earthquake raised the sea floor in some places by a few feet. An amazing surf break called Rags Right, which was always almost too shallow to surf safely became too dangerous to ride after the reef was lifted. Lugundi Bay to the far north became a better, more hollow wave.

Some breaks simply ceased to exist.

The Addiction's Skipper added a few new perspectives to this when recalling his discussions with other experienced surfers who have been coming to the Mentawais for years. They have observed that even without an obvious earthquake, parts of the coast move up and down slightly each year changing the surf breaks over time. Apparently, Rags Right has again started to be surfed as the uplifted zone has settled down a bit. It has been speculated that even the amazing HTs might not have even been a good surf spot a few centuries ago as the coastline there is gradually sinking. The name HTs came from a drowned hollow tree that used to stand in the shallows in from the reef, reflecting this movement. It was strange to think of a coast moving and shifting on a yearly basis – undulating almost like the ocean itself.

* * *

We motored from the mooring back to Lance's. Again solid, oily-surfaced blue swells rolled under The Addiction and surged off towards the distant coast to slam into reefs lining the shore. From the boat we could see these explosions and hear their dull roar as we travelled along the coast. A soft mist clung to the coast generated from the spray of the surf. The surf break soon appeared in the distance. It looked amazing. The waves were at least well overhead and still empty. We watched as three waves span off perfectly along the reef looking incredibly inviting. There was no wind at all.

After days on our own I was feeling a bit more secure

that we would not have a charter boat full of rabid surfers suddenly steam in to spoil our fun. In peak season, Lance's Lefts can have 3 to 4 boats on it all day which would be a nightmare as far as I was concerned. Catching a handful of leftover waves every hour was not why I had travelled to remote Sumatra. Nevertheless, watching empty perfect waves still made me edgy and nervous – they are too rare and precious to waste. I raced to hit the water as though I was back home trying to beat the hordes to a new swell.

The swell was a bit smaller than the day before and more settled, glassy and lined up. Skelts unfortunately had a problem to deal with. The day before, he had chosen not to wear booties, given that it had looked like a rolling chunky wave breaking well out from the shallow inside reef. Lance's Lefts' teeth, however, are still sharp, just tucked away out of sight. A nasty wipe-out and drag across the reef had left him in shallow water and Skelts' foot touched down briefly giving him some nasty cuts on the top of the foot behind his little toe.

Paul had leapt into action and done the essential cleaning and treatment from his bag of potions. This morning the cuts were still painful, oozing and deep enough to cause concern. As Skelts considered his options for the day, other tour members had plenty of advice.

Paul prescribed a sound regime of treatment and care: no surf for at least five days; daily treatment with antiseptic liquid and powder and of course nightly spinal board constriction in bed to minimise movement. Understandably, this was not what Dave wanted to hear. Hoover suggested using daily application of his cure-all horse liniment. Coops offered a rum and burnt incense poultice and texted his mystical mentor - Sting - for further advice. Taff showed his beaten up feet from 20 years of Tae Kwon Do in sympathy. In the end, Skelts did what any surf warrior would do and decided to grit his teeth and surf anyway. It would be more painful to have to sit and watch perfect overhead Lances Lefts from the boat. So he rigged up a glad wrap and bubble wrap protector for his foot and put his booties on over the top.

Tim, Paul and Hoover headed over to Bintangs for a pleasant session of fun peaks.

Lance's Lefts was peeling evenly from way over at the inside take-off right through to the inside section. The rides were 150 metres of glassy blue perfection. We sat right on the edge of the inside take-off this time which was a lot more settled than yesterday and took it in turns picking off waves. The swell was inconsistent again with long waits for 2-3 wave sets. Some sets had only one lonely wave. Such conditions told the story of the swell's origins. The storm that created them must have been from the furthest southern reaches of the Indian Ocean down below South Africa somewhere. As they march across thousands of miles of ocean, storm waves coalesce into long even sets and space out. Somehow over huge distances a further consolidation process occurs, perhaps with the weaker waves in sets slowly fading or merging with the bigger waves to form sets that could be ten or even fifteen minutes apart.

If conditions had been crowded this would have been very frustrating. If 20 people sit on a flat ocean for fifteen minutes and finally 3 waves turn up the maths of sharing just do not work. A lot of people have to miss out. It becomes survival of the fittest and the young guys inevitably picking off the gems.

For us, with only seven sharing the line up everything worked fine. Again, it was not a wave fest but there was the definite advantage when caught inside as it meant a two wave duck dive at worst and then an easy paddle into clear water and safety. A twenty wave set from a closer storm event would mean a trip over the reef after every wipe-out.

Dean was only one metre inside us this time and was much improved in his take-offs and surfing than the day before. He went hard for tubes but they avoided him and gave him numerous foam ball rides and head dips right in the pocket instead. Doug was surfing well confidently taking off on the peak and going for everything that moved. Taff also got some great waves and started to pull off some of his excellent patented backside cutbacks. Skelts had a frenzy of wave catching on the peak and inside to maximise his wave count in the shorter space of time he had allotted himself to avoid letting his cut get too soggy in the seawater.

We surfed in the morning heat for hours and slowly the tour members drifted back to the boat for a second breakfast. As always I stayed out savouring the empty lineup. My magic broad brimmed hat kept me cool between waves. It added hours to my surf time each day in surprising comfort even in the midday heat. It was like a little world of cool under the brim. On the last trip on a cloudless day, I had not been wearing a hat and felt like my face and head was frying in the sun the whole surf. I tried to hold my hand up to protect my face and even lay in the water using the surfboard as a shield. Nothing took the incredible burning glare away and I was ready to head back to the boat after an hour in spite of the quality waves. A surf hat became a priority for this trip. My trick was to quickly stuff in down the back of my rash vest, if I had time, or to flip it off the back, when I rode waves to avoid the distraction of the brim obscuring my peripheral vision.

The long waits for sets continued and I sat alone in a big blue ocean picking off a wave every ten minutes. Then a speed boat arrived from around the corner with 4 other surfers so I headed in as my grumbling stomach had been asking for lunch for a long time.

After a while, the boys came back from across the bay at Bintangs where they'd had a very pleasant morning's surf and the pick of the waves. I quizzed them on the wave quality getting mixed reports on size. I thought it would have been really small but was left confused as to how good it was. Taff and I decided to head over to see firsthand leaving Lances Lefts to the other boat and tour members for the moment. Geni pulled the dingy up next to the platform off the back of The Addiction and we climbed aboard cradling our surf boards and then hung on tight as we sped across the bay feeling the breeze in our faces and having another close look at the bombie.

Near the peak at Bintangs we leapt overboard enjoying the refreshing lukewarm water flush of water, climbed on our boards and paddled to the peak. The Bombie out the back was still breaking at size occasionally. Next thing we knew we were paddling over the shoulder of a sucky blue peak that was just as big as the day before. It was on again!

It turned out to be bigger and more consistent than the previous day at times for some reason despite the drop in overall swell size. The Bintangs reef and the bombie outside swung the swells around affecting angles and size as the waves curve into the little corner of the bay. Often the slightly smaller sets did not break properly on the outside Bombie and so reached the peak at maximum size. Weirdly, many of the biggest sets outside were smaller than the medium ones once they reached us.

In between waves we sat on our boards and absorbed the amazing scene around us. The palm-lined beaches swept left and right as shimmering white strips of coral sand ground from the reefs over many centuries by swells and the chomping of coral by trigger fish. The water was deep blue outside with lighter and darker shades coloured by reef and sand around us. Wind swung in eddies creating dead glass at times and offshore gusts at others patterning the water around the bay. Fish ducked in and out of the reef below our feet. Pointy nosed garfish poked their nose out of the water occasionally. Some splashes and flashes of fast moving silver fish broke the surface. Somewhere, in some other world, a billion people went about their business doing things we didn't know or care to know.

*  *  *

 For centuries the waves across the Mentawais, would have just come and gone, observed, but largely unappreciated (in the way surfers appreciate tem) by the locals. Many would have ridden them regularly in their canoes and outriggers coming into sheltered bays after fishing trips – a brief rush of speed and a time to rest paddles as the rising wave did some of the work. It would have been fun for them if the waves were gentle and a place to avoid on larger swells. I wondered if they ever paddled out just to do it for the pleasure in some gentler sloping waves. Perhaps here and there some did spend the morning catching waves in their canoe just for fun whilst the rest of the villages thought them crazy or wasteful of time?

Hawaii was a more natural place for surfing to evolve as a recreation, than the Mentawais, particularly around the Waikiki area. In the bay there waves break in long rollers from way out to sea over a myriad of reefs. Often they have gentle sloping faces for hundreds of metres. It would have been a foolish fisherman in a canoe who did not use them to speed up the last mile or so of the trip back from out to sea. From there it would be a small step to just riding them for their own sake and exploring other wave riding craft options.

Most Mentawai waves were, however,  a lot less inviting

to ride in something as clumsy as a canoe that those at Waikiki. On small days the bombie in the bay outside Bintags was one exception. It peaks up to feather briefly and then eases back into deep water unbroken – perfect for a brief speed run on a canoe.

Nowadays, quite a few of the local Mentawai kids surf on boards left by travelling surfers. The youngest often ride broken or repaired boards missing fins and noses. If it floats they will try to surf it. Whenever I saw any of them surfing I was struck by how much they seemed to enjoy it. They laughed and chatted with each other endlessly between waves. It was nice to see that surfing had added a whole new dimension to their isolated island lives.

* * *

Big sets at Bintangs would appear out of nowhere as concave valleys in the ocean, sucking over the reef inviting us to try to step *inside* the ocean for a moment or two. We traded waves pushing our turns and trying for some off-the-top moves and tube rides. Big cutbacks after the peak were fun and routine by now. The tube potential of the peak beckoned. We both started taking off right in the middle of the peak. I even stalled a few times. We had some great pocket rides and the lip flicked over our heads. Taff ended up getting a nice tube on the inside section where the reef ledges seemed to fill the bottom of the wave with a kaleidoscope of colours. Late in the surf I sneaked a neat little tube ride in there as well.

Geni came over with Tim, Paul and Hoover in the

tender and took photos. We paddled over and hung off the side of the boat to enjoy some delicious cool drinks from the ice box. I downed two boxes of juice and a can of some Indonesian energy drink before paddling back to the peak. Dehydration was something to avoid as I had learned on the last trip where after a seven hour surf without a drink I suffered the next day for my foolishness.

Late in the day, The Addiction came over and moored in the corner of the bay nearby. Taff and I surfed on and were joined by Doug and Charlie. The surf seemed to even pick up at this point but became a bit more fickle and hard to read. The tide had swung and was pulling us away from the peak and making the waves more chunky and uneven with the swirling current. Our strike rate fell off a bit but still some good waves were ridden. The swell pushed in harder and became more consistent but without the quality of earlier.

Three local surfers came out and paddled for everything that moved. We let them have the pick of the waves. One pulled off a backside tube where he came out of the barrel sitting on his board in full control, laughing with delight. The local boys caught most of the best waves though and chatted excitedly with each other in between sets. Clearly they were very familiar with the spot and loved their surfing.

Taff and Charlie went back to the boat and Doug and I surfed on. The waves cleaned up again and we got some nice rides. Our surf was brought to an end when Doug and I were caught inside by a multi wave set that just did not let up. Doug was closer to the channel and paddled hard and escaped after a bit of a struggle. I was pushed right into waist deep water into an awkward position. It was the sort of place where a leg could hit a lump of coral easily cutting soft waterlogged skin. It was too shallow to duck-dive and it was awkward to stand on the uneven coral. I paddled and paddled roughly keeping my place expecting a fin to get knocked out on a chunk of reef at any moment. Finally a let up occurred and I went hard for deep water. Both Doug and I saw this as a signal that it was time to head back to the boat.

We paddled a few hundred metres over the deep channel to the boat. Upon reaching the stern of The Addiction, I hauled myself up onto the lower platform. A hand held shower was there to rinse off with. I savoured the fresh, cool water as it washed away the salt that encrusted my hair, face and eyelashes. Next I staggered up the stairs to the lower deck feeling every bit my fifty years. My eyes were burning from salt and sun. I pulled off my shorts and rash vest and sat there, in a stupor of exhaustion, wrapped in a towel drinking juice and tried to work out how to ease the pain in my eyes.

Closing them hurt but so did holding them open. It felt like there was a sliver of sandpaper tucked under each eyelid. Eight hours of salty water dripping into my eyes had left its mark. The word from the other guys when they looked at the two glowing red holes above my nose was "scary". I tried eye drops to no avail. In the end, I found that if I blinked fast and often, I could confuse them and the nerves could not work out whether they hurt or not.

At this point in the trip we had to make some decisions on the future journey. The swell forecast was far from great. We were in for a prolonged stretch of small swells. The choice was either to go way down south to Thunders or up north to some swell magnets located there. The decision was made to head to a mooring near a very exposed left, called Scarecrows, for the night and then head north the next morning. We left the waves empty of surfers – a rare occurrence these days.

Our path took us around the lee side of the islands. Amazingly, in the middle of the boat trip in the dark, we came across the charter boat that had Hoover's precious lost board and bags placed there by arrangement in the hope our paths would cross at some point. A quick exchange was made and he finally had his magic new board and precious rucksack back again.

That night the T-shirt was awarded to Skelts for bravery and wounds sustained in the battle for Lance's Lefts. Dave had been first to suffer a dangerous injury through his devil may care approach to surfing. He had also impressed all by cutting short his prescribed time out of the water by 5 days and only missing the one surf the afternoon before due to the injury. Dave accepted his award nonchalantly as would be expected of someone so used to danger and gave a long speech about "important stuff".

I hit the bunk early in a state of exhaustion and tried to sleep with one eye still painful and weeping from exposure to salt and sun (or perhaps it was the horse liniment emanating in a cloud from the sleeping Hoover on the top bunk). Taff stayed up with Coops and had a dangerous session of Rum nips, re-birthing experiences and deep philosophising.

Taff looked reborn, or perhaps very hung over, the next morning, as he stood watching the sunrise with a mystical, faraway look in his eye. A half expected to see a crystal clenched in his palm and hear the waft of Coops' favourite mood music - the Songs of the Humpback Whale coming from his cabin.

**Skelts at Karangniki**

Clive M. Woodward

# 4. SHARKS – OF DEITIES AND DANGERS

**What lurks below?**

When Dean invited me on my first trip to the islands, one of my first questions was, "what about sharks". He assured me that there were no sharks there. That was seemed a little too good to be true. Of course, I hopped onto the internet to find out more. After hunting around various websites I was left with the impression that they were in fact quite scarce and rarely seen. A few spots, however, did appear to have occasional visits from some large Tiger Sharks.

My first leap off the charter boat into deep water felt a bit strange but after a while paddles back to the boat over deep water and sitting alone off a remote coral reef over unseen marine life was a routine part of the day. The Skipper could only recall seeing one in the surf in over five years I was very pleased to hear. The region has been heavily fished for the last century feeding locals and the heavily populated nearby South East Asian region. Whilst fish life was visible when we surfed it was nothing like the volume of fish around islands in the tropics that humans rarely visited.

It was common to see small schools of colourful reef fish swimming around the coral whilst we surfed. Often some large blue fish could be seen deep beneath the boat when we were anchored. These were not the appetising silver-sided pelagic or reef fish that seemed appealing to my tastes and I suspect sharks felt the same way. Game fish could sometimes be caught when trolling between islands. But, I never saw the swirling masses of school fish that feature in documentaries set in coral atolls. Food was relatively scarce and so too were the predators. We all knew sharks were out there among the reefs we frequented but they appeared scarce enough to justify feeling comfortable in the water.

Surfers everywhere spend thousands of hours living with a sense of vulnerability as they enjoy their sport. We all live with the thought that at any time a dark shadow or a fin cutting the surface could turn a playful frolic into one of life's most primeval struggles. Attacks are rare. However, with the internet as a medium to share stories, it is amazing to note how common it is for surfers to see sharks. Forums with topics along the lines of "saw a shark today" soon fill with shared stories. Mostly these are a mention of a brief glimpse of a long dark shadow or a fin. Sometimes they tell of bumps and nudges from curious sharks. Occasionally someone describes a genuine pursuit. I read recently where a shark chased a surfer into the rocks and then ended up thrashing briefly on a rock ledge as it beached itself in desperation to catch the surfer who had scrambled out of the water only seconds before.

For a handful of surfers each year around the world the outcome is much more serious. As I write, another surfer has been killed in Western Australia, the ninth attack there in 5 years.

The endless sightings and encounters documented on the internet have dispelled a long held view I had throughout my prime surfing years that sharks were relatively scarce. I have only personally had a few sightings. Off Snapper Rocks in Queensland I saw one early one morning when I was out surfing by myself on a small day (an impossible feat you would think given the constant crowd there). It was about 100 metres away lazily cruising out to sea.

I headed into the rocks once in a hurry at a Tasmanian left point after seeing something dark thrashing in the kelp covered rocks – but headed out again soon after as the waves were too much fun to leave. Other than that there was maybe a fin once that I did not stick around to confirm and lot of splashing among the birds feeding on fish way out to sea one other time that I thought suspicious.

Now that I know that encounters with surfers are relatively common, I am both more wary but also more re-assured. In general, the evidence is very clear that in the vast majority of situations they wander past and leave us alone.

Those who cannot get used to living with this risk probably quit the sport or never start. The rest of us live with it and manage our fears - usually by our choices of surf spot. We all avoid some places or visit them only rarely when conditions are too perfect to resist.

The degree of comfort and actual risk varies a great deal with the reputation of where you surf and the circumstances on the day. Some places feel spooky – usually for good reason. Or else they have a history of attacks or aggressive encounters. On a sunny day, with a crowd of other surfers around, thoughts of sharks barely crosses your mind. On a grey, overcast day at an isolated spot by yourself, they can play on your mind to the point where the fun goes out of the session and you quietly paddle in leaving good waves un-surfed.

I have talked to some oil rig workers who are based off the northwest coast of Western Australia, away from any significant fishing activity, about the sharks that surround the rigs. The general view was that if you fell off the rig, you would not last five minutes in the water due to the number of aggressive sharks that hang around the pylons.

At Reunion Island off Africa, they have recently closed much of the coast to surfing after a string of horrific attacks. The local surfers think these are a direct result of the creation of marine reserves long the coast that have been very successful in creating a huge surge in the fish population. Apparently the population of Tiger Sharks and Bull Sharks has increased in equal proportion. With safety in numbers, the sharks have become much more aggressive and the recent attacks were not exploratory bites. The sharks were bent on killing and eating their prey.

At Bikini Atoll, where mankind has rarely visited for the half century since the test of the early atomic bombs, a visiting underwater photographer a decade ago filmed an incredible profusion of fish and sharks within the lagoons. Without any fishing pressure from humans the ocean can explode with life quite quickly. He also noted that the population of Tiger Sharks was very aggressive and feared nothing. They roamed around attacking everything in sight, including him until he retreated to his boat. Whilst, of course, they may be in the process of mutating into some horrific new predator due to radiation exposure, the more likely cause of this aggression is their sheer numbers and placement at the top of the food chain without man around to give them cause to fear anything else.

The degree of safety we have come to accept as normal when surfing and undertaking many other aquatic pursuits is not necessarily the permanent state of things or something that is the same across the planet. Statistics only tell part of the story.

Sydney, Australia, for example, was renowned for shark attacks early last century until meshing started to cull their numbers near popular swimming beaches. The theory was that shark numbers were high and many had established territories where they felt comfortable and defensive. Bondi recorded many attacks until long nets strung out to sea broke the pattern.

Now, after a long period of safety for beach loving Australians, risks may be on the rise. Since Great White sharks have been protected, surfers and fishermen have noticed large populations of juvenile Great Whites developing along beaches north of Newcastle above Sydney at certain times of year. At two metres long, these are still focusing on rays, fish and other small sharks for food. California is seeing the same trend. In another decade they will be full grown and looking for bigger prey. The Reunion Island experience has shown how quickly the dynamics and behavior patterns can change.

Islanders across the Pacific and Indian oceans have varied widely in their relationship with the ocean and sharks. Hawaiians famously pioneered surfing and made being in, on and around the ocean a major part of their lives. Their culture and beliefs placed sharks as revered and respected creatures, creating a sense of safety when swimming or surfing. The long rolling gentle waves of Waikiki Beach, and these beliefs, were an ideal combination encouraging the islanders to step out of their canoes and onto carved wooden boards to ride waves.

Today, Hawaiians by ancestry, who refer to sharks as Mano, turn the traditional surfers' view of sharks on its head by believing that their Mano watch and protect them. The sharks are the embodiment of gods and family deities called "aumakua" and are seen as part of the family.

Shark are often seen in Hawaii, particularly on the South

Shore. Accounts and mentions of sightings of Tiger Sharks have, over the years, been common enough, without incident, that some of their aura as dangerous predators had faded. This fostered a sense of security among locals and visitors alike. Attacks, however, have recently become more common, partly blamed on large increase in the green sea turtle population following its protection. The reaction has been a mixture of shock and surprise. It was in Hawaii, after all, where the relationship between water goers and sharks was supposed to be different.

Despite this, the traditional Hawaiian view is that they never intentionally attack the ethnic Hawaiians who pay them proper respect. On a recent forum online some discussions on the topic ensued after a surfer was attacked. A Hawaiian responded that he often knew when they were near and felt protected by their presence. Another local noted with annoyance that when a Tiger Shark cruised by in the line-up where he surfed it was the non-Hawaiians that made turned it into a dangerous situation by panicking or becoming nervous and agitated. As a Hawaiian, he would stay calm and give respect to the visitor and let it pass on and have no trouble. Deity or not, this sense of calmness on its own, would have a protective role as sharks respond to fear. Even so, another contributor noted that the crowds at local south shore spots had tended to thin more than previously around 45 minutes before sunset since the recent attacks. Fear creeps up in mild increments even on the most blasé in the dim light of the setting sun.

A long time ago, on a stopover back from Europe, I

paddled way out to sea off Waikiki beach on a hire board to ride some waves. I was alone out there except for one other surfer in a vast arena of shifting peaks. At the time, my knowledge of the shark population was limited. All I knew was that the local Hawaiians did not worry about them. I surfed away fairly calmly for a few hours in prime Tiger Shark territory protected not by my personal Mano deity but by my ignorance and luck.

In contrast, in the Gilbert Islands, in the south Pacific, early last century, male Tiger Sharks were hunted for their genitals purported power as an aphrodisiac. The locals regarded the aggressive Tiger Shark as dangerous but slow witted. A rite of passage for the young men was to kill a large male shark in single combat armed with just a knife. This ritual is described by an eye witness, Arthur Grimble, in his classic tale of life as an employee of the British Colonial office in *A Pattern of Islands*. One morning he was taken out in a canoe to watch as a young man, eager to pursue a romantic interest and prove his manhood, took on a shark.

They went to the mouth of the lagoon where a large group of Tiger Sharks endlessly patrolled hunting food that passed in and out with the currents and tides. After spotting a large shark the young man jumped overboard with a knife in one hand and faced his adversary. By nature, the Tiger Sharks in that lagoon apparently had a pattern of caution, where they would circle for a while before a sudden direct charge straight at their prey. They could be scared away completely if a swimmer swam went directly at them. Grimble's life was saved by this very strategy when his canoe capsized and the local boy with him swam through the line of Tiger Sharks to get help. He repeatedly had to swim directly at the sharks when their curiosity had turned to aggression over and over until he finally reached shallow water.

Grimble watched the duel with fascination as the slow dance of the two adversaries began. The shark circled as did the young man ensuring that he faced it at all times. Eventually the shark made its move. In that instant the islander swum quickly sideways and down under water, reached up with his knife and sliced the shark's softer belly wide open. He then waited for it to complete its death throes, staining the surrounding water with deep red blood. Once it went belly up he sliced off the prized male claspers. What struck Grimble most about the whole event was the casual nature of the young man afterwards. He was very pleased to have secured such a large set of claspers and to have proven his mettle in battle but regarded the whole adventure as almost routine – just part of life.

The Gilbert Islanders comfort in the ocean was further illustrated by their novel way of catching large octopus that live in the ledges of deep coral reefs. Working in pairs, once they spotted a few legs poking out of a crack, one boy would jump down into the water as bait and let the octopus come out and wrap all its legs around him ready for a meal. He would then float to the surface and roll on his back so that the octopus was out of the water on his chest. The second boy would grab it and somehow push its head through its body turning it inside out! Somehow they knew the octopus would not use its sharp beak immediately.

Our assumptions about shark behavior are slowly
changing. A French diver in South Africa has
demonstrated that even with the feared Great White, it
is possible to manage a free dive, unprotected by a cage
with very large sharks. The amazing film available on
the internet shows him hanging in space, face to face
with some huge sharks. He even grabs a dorsal fin and
lets s shark pull him along. Like a Lion Tamer, he
knows that calm and confidence, is his protection. The
diver picks his playmates though as some visitors to his
boat are cranky and aggressive and best left alone.

Near Farallon Island off San Francisco, a man called
Ron, dives unprotected for sea urchins in an area full of
Great Whites. His story is told in the book *Devils Teeth*
by Susan Casey. He has the pick of the best urchins for
the Japanese market as he is the only person game
enough to dive there. His strategy is to always dive
directly beneath his boat so that none of the local sharks
ever see his dark silhouette against the bright sea
surface. His only tool of defense is his bag of urchins
which, if harassed, he will push the shark away with or
shove into its mouth. To him they are manageable
nuisances.

Before we get too blasé about them, however, it is
worth noting the behavior Jim Shekhdar, a British ocean
rower who was the first person to complete a solo
unassisted non-stop crossing of the Pacific, saw in mid
ocean from a number of large Great Whites. In deep
ocean food is fairly scarce and these sharks seemed very
hungry and very determined to get at Jim. They had
eyed him off on a cruise past a clearly say him as food.

Repeatedly they lined up his boat from about 30 metres away and charged it at full speed ramming it with their heads. They ignored the pain this caused and Jim's jabs with his spear and spent a good half hour battering his boat to no aval.

For the surfer and shark management this means that in the end sharks can be seen as neither friend nor foe. Generally the dangers they present are low and in many cases declining through overfishing. We all just need to understand that the dynamics can change in particular localities over time and not base decisions on broad brush statistics taken across hugely diverse marine environments. Oddly, I am now more wary of shark dangers in Australia than Indonesia.

Whilst on the boat I, of course, kept all such musings and thoughts of sharks out of my mind. The topic was never really mentioned among us by unspoken agreement. Nevertheless, my own casual observations of the sea life and the views of experienced veterans of the Mentawais, made it reasonable to assume we surfed in a zone with a relatively high degree of safety. Nonetheless, only once, did I stay in the water late into the evening.

Clive M. Woodward

# 5. SWELL MAGNETS

**The Author at Karangniki Island**

I was up early the next day keen to check out the conditions. In semi darkness on deck, Tim sat gazing into the distance at the vague smudges of coastline slowly becoming visible in the early light. The mooring looked a bit familiar and I was pretty sure it was where we spent the night two years before after a great day surfing Scarecrows. The outline of the island in from the surf break was visible in the early morning light. My memories of it were as a classic round tropical island surrounded by a brilliant white beach and crowned with a stand of coconut palms. Hidden in the groves was a resort of sorts where a surfer with a sculptor's eye had created an amazing home largely out of driftwood and polished timber. Shells and interesting ocean flotsam were woven into the fabric of the building. It was as though Tom Bombadill from *The Lord of the Rings* had set up his home in the forest awaiting passing Hobbits. The owner lived there part of the year and the rest of the time in Hawaii – a testament to the remarkable life choices possible in this world if you step outside the mainstream.

The crew was up and getting ready to set off for the day. Downstairs Tony was doing his morning routine of cutting up a tropical fruit platter for breakfast. The Skipper was also checking the conditions and commented that the never-too-small Scarecrows was not working at all. Icelands up the coast would hopefully be bigger. It was a worrying sign as the swell had to be really low for Scarecrows to be too small to surf.

I kept watching as we began to head north. A small set hit and a perfect series of lefts peeled across the reef. They might have been waist high but it was hard to tell from a distance in the misty dawn light. I felt like saying we should go for a closer look but the momentum was north and I was sure Icelands would have some size. Slowly the rest of the tour members came up on deck to check out the day. The lack of swell was very apparent to all. We could barely notice any swell lines passing under the boat.

Further north we came across where a famous surf break called Telescopes was supposed to be. Some tiny waves dribbled across the reef giving no hint that this was one of the best lefts in the world when it was on. The apt name of Telescopes derived from the visual symmetry of the multiple long tubular swells the massive horseshoe-like reef created as it curved them around the reef. On my last trip there we surfed it a couple times and late one evening after a glass off, it turned into an endless spinning pipe that mesmerised as it steamed in from way up the reef. The first kilometre was too fast to make. Then, not far from where we sat the curve of the reef created a surfable peeling end section for 200 metres. Sadly, today, it gave no hint of its potential.

We headed around the corner to Icelands – a left named because of the iceberg-like aqua blue hue to the water. Again, there was no hint of what it could do on a good day. Small fat peaks broke into a channel. One of the Mentawai swell magnets, supposed to always have size, was about as flat as it gets. After a ten minute check with nothing of interest to see we set off again for a long trip up north to one of the more northerly swell magnets – Burgerworld.

It took a bit of faith to believe that there would be swell up there but it was always known to never be flat. Burgerworld was high on my list as a performance right and so I was happy with the move and hoped for some classic point waves later in the morning.

It was quite pleasant to actually be able to sit around on deck and rest the body and mind by doing nothing much and watch the ocean roll by. I had pretty much been surfing or eating and nothing else in the day time for the past three days. Flying fish would zoom across the waves periodically and I saw a small Marlin jump briefly in the wake at one point highlighting how alive the ocean was. Tour members spread themselves out to relax. Tim set a long line out the back to try to catch some game fish. No-one said much, as we sat lost in our own thoughts, enjoying a pause in the action and the passive pleasure of watching the Catamaran cut through the deep blue sea.

Burgerworld came into view much sooner than expected. The Addiction was making full use of its speed capabilities and we had made amazing time. We reached there by mid-morning when most other charter boats would have taken most of the day to make the journey. From a distance the size looked good. The swell was somehow hitting up this end of the island chain in long even lines. I never could quite work out how the swell at Icelands could be tiny and Burgerworld could be well overhead on the sets on the same day. It highlighted again how waves are really just energy pulses not unlike the beam of a torch. They head out to where they are directed by the dominant wind direction in the storm, spreading out to a degree over time. But step outside the direct path of the beam and you will soon be in darkness. Burgerworld or the less demeaning local name of Karangniki Island was clearly directly in the beam of light from some distant storm.

The name "Burgerworld" is one of the most inappropriate surf spot name choices I've ever come across. It deserves far better. The island is just picture perfect with the most scenic backdrop you can imagine of palm trees intermingled with dense tropical foliage right down to the water's edge. Waves peeling down the island reminding one of Noosa or a north NSW coast point up to about 5 foot. A beautiful little beach lies on the leeward side of the island leading to a less dense area of vegetation and a couple of huts hidden deep in the foliage. On the other side of the island an un-named left peeled for a couple of hundred metres mostly ignored and un-ridden.

Being very keen to get stuck into a long right hand point break, I was ready to hit the water as soon as we moored. It was a bit too big and chunky to be its best. A-frame peaks broke randomly here and there along the point – some with walls and some going fat. It was very similar to a somewhat frustrating day I had surfing there two years before. The wave was best on smaller swells. On the plus side, it was sunny, glassy and empty.

The surf turned out to be better than expected. A lot of peaks had good walls and the big takeoffs were fun. It was hard work to catch the peaks. To do so you had to be prepared to sit where stray big outside sets would break rolling through and over you with powerful white water. We all did a lot of duck diving under solid waves as we held our spot for the medium sets. I spent many duck dives underwater that day hanging on to my board, sometimes in control, often upside down, trying to punch through rolling walls of white water from broken waves.

Skelts paddled into the inside near the point where some waves peeled in excellent long walls occasionally between the bigger sweeping masses of white water. He picked up some good ones in there, although, it looked hard work for the waves he caught. I picked some nice waves from partway down the point that peeled well. Taff and the others also hung out there getting good waves. At other times I headed right out the back to the tip of the point where some solid overhead peaks would come through giving big take-offs and sometimes a huge horseshoe section to follow with amazing speed and power.

Supposedly "soft" Burgerworld gave us all the hardest physical workout of the entire trip. It felt like a big wild beach break at times as we dodged the random outside peaks. After a long surf, we drifted back to the boat with a reasonable amount of daylight left in the day. The next stop overnight was to be the Playgrounds area – an amazing series of set ups in close proximity to one another a half hour's motor away. We sped off with a detour planned on the way for Nipussi's – a very good right-hander with long walls that are powerful but not ferocious.

Nipussi's was the first stop on my first trip in 2010. It was also my first proper surf over a coral reef. After a few surfs in 2ft beach breaks in the lead up to the trip I was nervous at first and then shocked by the power when a set of about five solid waves caught me inside early in the surf. After escaping out the back I sat in the channel wide eyed and breathless wondering what I had let myself in for.

On that surf, I watched a lot of waves peak way over on the start of the reef as well as in the middle and across at the end nearer the channel where I sat. Peaks would swing in from a range of angles and hit the reef potentially catching you off-guard but also offering a number of take-off spots. From my safer spot near the channel I had particularly eyed off the far peak which gave the longest ride across the whole reef. Thinking about the wave afterwards I came to realise that it was the prime spot to sit and was really just as "safe" as anywhere if the swell was not too consistent. I checked a few videos of Nipussis and this showed the far inside peaks as some of the best ones to catch

We arrived at Nipussis to find it empty. This was far from normal given that it is a very consistent spot close to land resorts and a popular place for boats to visit. My guess was that it was a bit overhead but that was hard to judge from the back of the wave. There was not much wind around, just a few puffs of side-shore breeze every now and then. Tour members peered in at the wave for a bit but given that it was overhead and empty, there was really no decision to be made. The deck became a frenzy of people in the familiar routine of getting the gear on, smearing sunblock on faces and legs and waxing up boards. I took out my McCoy half expecting it to surprise us, as it tends to, by being bigger than it looked.

After being dropped off by the tender, I watched a set go by from the shoulder checking it all out and then paddled way over to my inside take-off spot on faith that peaks would pop up and waited. The rest of the guys were a bit further over where most peaks were focusing. The waves were hard to catch as they often

97

backed off a bit after looking really promising out the back.  Early in the surf a bigger set peaked over where I was and I just caught it and had a long exciting drop followed by a fast ride across the bay. It was a great wave and very satisfying that a memory from two years ago had put me in the zone to catch it.  I went back to my spot while the other guys got busy catching the peaks inside a bit.  The waves in there were solid fun walls and from the chat afterwards it was clear they picked up some good rides. My patience was rewarded by two more sizeable waves.  For a brief while I thought it was going to be outstanding surf.  After that everything I paddled for backed off.  I stuck to my guns in my "secret spot" but never caught another wave. After about a half hour or so a speed boat with 4 other surfers turned up.  I paddled away to the channel figuring I would stick with the memory of my three good waves rather than join the fray inside. I waved my board to signal for a pick up and was picked and headed back to the boat.  Everyone soon made the same decision and left the fortunate newcomers with an un-crowded surf.

It was a short motor to the Playgrounds mooring past more idyllic (but probably mindlessly hot in the afternoon sun) tropical islands lined by long white sandy beaches.  At our mooring we were within sight of one of the world's best selections of surf spots in close proximity anywhere.  To our left was Nokanduis – a super-fast left that can produce 12 second tubes on a solid swell.  Today it was just a dribble.  To the right was Chubbies, a right, breaking around a sand island. Chubbies is termed a longboarders wave but this is something Charlie would debate as he once had a two wave hold down there when the horseshoe end section slammed down on him. In the distance was A-frames, a quality left with a great peak and wall. It looked about 4 foot as best I could judge from a long distance away. To the right of this was Four Bobs, a super fun right-hander. In the far distance was Kanduis or Rifles, a long right that was viewed as one of the world's best waves by many when the right swell direction hit it. Finally, just in front of the mooring was a reef with a long left peeling away known to be a fun wave perfect for cruising on a long board. To all of us that evening it looked pretty well perfect at perhaps waist to shoulder high. It was a smorgasbord of possibilities. The area must have blown the minds of the first surfers to discover it. There are so many quality waves in a compact area and somewhere is good or excellent every day of the year. It was getting dark quickly so all we could do is watch and hope for the swell to hold overnight.

Tim was super keen to hit the small left the next day or perhaps Four Bobs. It looked just like some of Tasmania's river mouth breaks and was perfect shape and looked fun to surf. Dean and I had our eye on A-frames. It had a great wall for big turns and broke in fairly deep water for the most part. Hopes were high for the next day as there would be waves to suit everyone. The only dampener on spirits was the persistent forecast of small swells for the coming few days.

To avoid crowds, our trip was timed for early in the

season before the Southern Ocean had really become active with storms and cold fronts pushing swell up towards the equator. Early autumn could have some solid swells but there was always a chance of an extended stretch of low swell. That is what seemed to be heading our way. Thankfully the swell magnets sat waiting in the wings if needed.

The evening meal was excellent as usual – the amount of meat we were served always astounded me. I expected lots of rice and a bit of meat or fish. The lamb and beef we had a few times was superb. Best of all, I could go back for seconds and thirds knowing it would all get burned up the next day in the surf.

After dinner we settled down for some quiet drinks. I got chatting to Tim who proceeded to tell me a few wild stories of his West Coast life in a fishing town north of Perth. They made my office bound existence seem pretty tame. Some shall never be repeated. One was of dodging 20 foot breaking waves in the cray boat on the way back into a narrow harbour. Others were of ridiculous drunken escapades.

One story makes me wince to recall. Tim was on a boat with a very tough German skipper. A young guy was working with Tim and the skipper helping them launch the dingy through the shore break of a beach to head out to the cray boat to go and pull pots. The young guy was in bare feet and trod on a nasty fish native to the area that lives in the shallows. It has a sharp barbed spine that sticks straight up a few inches just below its head. A spike from this spine was intensely painful and usually meant a trip to hospital to extract it and a week off work.

The Skipper had other ideas. He had pots to pull. He took a good look at the young guy's foot with an inch of spine sticking out of the skin and another inch or so imbedded deep into the soul of his foot. He then got his big paw of a hand and slammed it hard into the spine driving it right up into the guy's foot so it was not sticking out anymore to catch on anything as he walked. The guy screamed in incredible pain. The Skipper just grunted "Now we work". The poor guy had to work the rest of the day on the boat with the crushed spine in his foot.

It is tough out there in the Wild West.

Later on Hoover told an even more harrowing story. He had been diving in Bass Strait of an isolated island somewhere and failed to decompress properly. Just after sunset he felt the onset of every diver's nightmare - the bends. If it set in fully he knew he would be in terrible pain and suffer lasting damage to his body or even death as nitrogen bubbles formed in his blood. He was 100 kilometres from a decompression chamber. Hoover took the only action he could. He put his wetsuit back on, grabbed a mask, two weight belts and a full air bottle and jumped overboard into the cold dark ocean.

Hoover let the heavy lead belts pull him to the sea floor where he found the anchor stuck in the sand. He clung to it and waited for the bubbles in his blood to subside. Alone and blind to his surroundings, he had to sit there in Great White Shark territory for what seemed like a very long time. Then it got worse. On the bottom he felt a little less exposed, but now Hoover had to do a staged decompression up the anchor chain. Slowly he moved up the chain pausing for long periods suspended in space wondering what might be swimming around him. As he told the story, we all felt a cold shiver go down our spines despite the warmth around us.

That night the winner of the T-Shirt was Doug - the true gentleman of the Tour members. He was fearless in the surf, deceptively fit and was neck and neck with rival Charlie in the surf hour tally for the trip so far. Doug had impressed day after day in the surf by casually swinging around and taking on the biggest and meanest sets with but a brief an analytical glance and a few strokes of his long arms. A couple of his long lefts at Lances from way inside were amongst the best waves of the trip.

We watched the distant waves peeling away all around us until it was too dark to see. There were high hopes for excellent surf the next day.

**Doug on one of the waves of the trip at Thunders**

Clive M. Woodward

# 6. KARANGNIKI BURGERS

I awoke predawn and lay in my bunk trying to sense if the swell had risen at all. Playgrounds offered so much potential for all the Tour Members that I was hoping for a swell increase more than any other day of the trip so far.

Our anchorage was sheltered by three islands and various reefs but was still subject to a roll from residual swells. In semi-darkness I waited for some hint that the swell had picked up. I lay there almost willing it to happen. My supernatural powers were not up to the task. There was nothing but the faintest roll. I went out on deck and joined Tim in checking the ocean. The vague lines I could make out in the pre-dawn light looked very small. The fun looking left nearby was peeling but without the hint of size of the night before. It was probably breaking too close to the reef to be safe.

A-frames looked to be barely breaking. Chubbies was flat as well.

Tim was still keen to surf in the Playgrounds area and there were definitely going to be waves. However, the problem would be that if it was small and inconsistent the few sets would have a swarm of surfers from other boats and the shore camps out chasing them. Dean, Charlie and Doug emerged on deck and the talk quickly turned to Burgerworld. It had been a bit too big for the point to handle well the day before but could be just right today. It was perfectly set up for head high waves. I was very keen to surf it good on this trip. Dean, Charlie, Doug, Skelts and Paul had all surfed dreamy Queensland point style waves in 2011 and were up for more. The crew was preparing to make a quick move and the Skipper confirmed that our best option was Burgerworld. We were soon off in the early dawn light at top speed to get ahead of any other boats.

The day was superb. Blue sky swept from horizon to horizon and there was virtually no wind. The Addiction cut through the water like a knife on its mission to give us more perfect surf. We ate some breakfast and then sat up on deck watching the blue water sweep by. Towards the island the swell lines became noticeable again to my relief. I had begun to wonder if the swell had gone completely. We had swell, no wind and were heading for a perfect point with no other boats in sight.

\* \* \*

My keenness to surf Burgerworld needs some
explanation. By the time I reached my late thirties I had
experienced my share of excellent surf mainly in
Tasmania and in Victoria where I lived for a few years. I
also surfed Queensland at its best on a number of trips.
Occasionally, Tasmania gets very good surf so I had
surfed perfect waves by any definition. Unfortunately,
our best set ups all seem to be tucked away from the
swell and need large swells from specific directions to
work. This is often a source of frustration; however, to
put it in perspective, at least I can name numerous world
class waves within an hour or two from where I live.
Some I have surfed better than anything I've seen in the
Mentawais so far. But the good days can be years apart.

The most technically perfect wave I've ever ridden was
Little Swanport (a left sandbar river mouth break deep
in a sheltered bay) in the late 1990s. It was slightly
overhead and every wave was virtually identical to the
one before. They peeled with a cartoonlike evenness
without even a hint of variability in the lip line or speed
of pitch so they looked like still photos as the tubes
spun off down the line. I remember paddling out
laughing at how ridiculously perfect every wave was as it
did not seem real.

Often, though, surfing in Tasmania on weekends, I felt
like a golf player who played mostly on overgrown and
poorly kept courses or a tennis player trying to make the
most of a cracked old weed-strewn court. The best
surfers can, of course, make something out of nothing
and turn even average surf into a high performance

session. As a mere mortal I needed more length and predictability to do good moves – a bit of time to set things up and get in a rhythm. I headed to Burgerworld that morning - one of the often derided spots in the Mentawais – with genuine excitement. Burgerworld lining up at 3-5ft would be pure fun.

\* \* \*

Once we motored in close we all knew it was on. The point was peeling away much more evenly and close to the rocks on the best part of the reef this time. Whilst it could get better, it was very good. For the moment it was just The Addiction crew there to surf it. Waves peaked out near the end pinnacle of rock that sticks like a bowsprit off the end of the island and peeled down the point reminiscent of T-Tree Bay at Noosa.

I think all the Tour Members felt the same about this surf as I did. It was low stress, easy to ride, plenty of waves and a canvas we could all paint freely upon. It was a lot of fun. Coops felt right at home. It was 1969 again and young Pete was out at Noosa with a few mates and Bob McTavish without a care in the world. Coops caught lots of waves and pulled off some excellent Pizza Man off the top slashes drenching me and others in the spray as well as other hand jive moves too innovative to name.

Dave, Skelts, Charlie and Paul seemed to have a new sense of aggression and were clearly pushing their surfing harder - perhaps inspired by some discussions we had on the boat about foot placement, use of arms and surf technique. Taff and I had been working on breaking old habits and had taken the challenge of trying to improve our surfing in our fifties. The Sydney boys were definitely now doing the same.

Dave sat right near the outside rocks in the prime spot for long fast waves right across the point. He caught some excellent waves there and was doing strong bottom and top turns. He looked like the young Skelts of thirty years ago ripping up a north coast point. Doug would sit in the same area in Zen Master Mode and stare the waves into submission before swinging around at the last minute to take off. He would then do full "Ming" bottom turns followed by "Sun Tzu" off the tops down the line. Charlie surfed solidly in the pocket and weaved up and down tucking into a few tubes. Paul sat inside and really got to work making up for lost time by catching anything wide or missed, surfing all over the wave with his steady, stylish hot dog moves.

Dean was doing his classic off the bottom followed by the big heavy backside slash creating a side wave and massive fan of spray. Dean also displayed big man style and poise in a new backside tube stance that he must have spent the winter secretly practicing in the mirror.

Taff, like me, was enjoying the opportunity to go hard off the bottom and carve off the top. He was also working on getting his cutback technique even more perfect to reach black belt status. I tested out my speed weave technique, did some nice cutbacks, sat in the pocket of a few tubes and started aiming for the lip every chance I got. I re-learned how to eye off the point where the lip throws out and aim for that spot rather than tucking in for a pocket ride or racing out to do a cutback. It felt great to really go all over the wave with a sense of freedom to carve at will.

Meanwhile, Hoover sat in amongst the crowd largely ignored, catching nothing. But, occasionally some inner urge stirred him into action and he decided a wave was his. When this happened, it was a sight to behold. A frothing storm would disturb the line up parting the crowd as he picked up speed chasing the poor unsuspecting wave.

His best wave this day was one of the waves of the trip and I had the privilege to see half of it. The early part was captured on film but the fastest part was not. By the time Mark reached me he was sitting at the top of the wave about a foot below the feathering lip in full speed trim. Just the thinnest edge of his board held him weightless in the wave face of the wave in a highline race through a long fast section. I'd like to say he was fully in control and cruising but as he passed me he face was a mask of concentration and his bung front leg was visibly shaking. Hoover swept by and down the point leaving a strong waft of horse liniment behind him.

Tim, at last, had a long righthander to show his longboard style and sweeping cutbacks. With wave spotting help from Paul and any other firend nearby, Tim caught some great waves.

We were each reveling in our fantasies of surfing Crescent Head, Snapper Rocks and Noosa back before they became crowded.

After a while, another boat arrived, making things a bit busier. But fortunately everyone shared a similar attitude and caught plenty of waves. I stayed out till well after lunch surfing through the hotter, but quieter, lunch period.

\* \* \*

After lunch I took a brief detour from my surf and eat schedule and was dropped off at the beach to do some shell collecting. Surfing all the time may seem a pretty one-dimensional holiday but this was by choice for all of us. On other family holidays we had our share of more traditional tourist activities where you "look at stuff". Here, our pleasures were unashamedly selfish and specialized.

Stones polished by centuries of wave action and interesting shells have long been my souvenir of choice at places I visit. On the beach there were a myriad of shells and broken pieces of sun-bleached coral. Hundreds of hermit crabs shuffled around in their commandeered shells. I spent a pleasant hour wandering along the water line, feet cooling periodically in the small surges of water that swept up the beach. I was mostly picking up tiny shells that were easy to travel with. They tended to have the brightest colours and most intricate designs. Cowries were common. Occasionally I would find tiny miniature Marble Cone shells, tiny failures in the battle for life, that were as yet unworn by the sea.

I glanced inland a few times from a distance to look to

where a family lived in a small hut in amongst the palms. They ignored the endless stream of surfers who visited the waters around their island. Whilst I was curious about their life, I had no wish to go closer to become a gawking tourist. I found my miniature souvenirs, signaled to be picked up and left them to their seclusion.

Cruising around the islands with limited contact with the local inhabitants may appear elitist and isolated. To me, however, it is more respecting of their culture than wandering through their villages uninvited. Surfers' touch on the islands is generally light. We do, however, contribute a tax to their local chiefs, buy some food and on occasional and even help out with a tow for a broken down fishing boat lost out to sea (as happened on our last trip). Land based resorts provide a lot of employment to locals. We do not tend to intrude on their daily village lives or culture in an attempt to "experience it" for our gratification or photographic trophies.

* * *

That night Bintang time saw some tired and happy surfers. It was Charlie's last night as he had to fly off on a mission to present to the board of his employer in Germany and so we all planned to celebrate his presence on the trip and his future absence (meaning still more waves for us). I think we all went to bed that night with a huge sense of satisfaction from five days of good surf and with anticipation for tomorrow. The trip was a success by any measure already and we still had five days to go.

The plan was to surf the island again and then head
south to drop off Charlie at a port where he had a speed
boat booked to take him to Padang. We would then
head for Macaronis - a left that could deliver everything
one could wish for in a wave.

**Charlie at Lance's Lefts**

Clive M. Woodward

# 7. ATOLLS OF THE SUN

I often thought about what it must be like to live on the island of Karangniki. Surfers only visit in small swells when five foot waves were normal fare. On medium swells it would have large walls rolling down both sides of the island. In large swells it would be huge and wild for days on end. To live there would mean endlessly hearing the roar of the ocean on all sides. For much of the peak swell season it would seem like living in a permanent storm.

Being a mere speck of island in a huge tsunami prone ocean would prey on one's mind if it was your home. However, the recent tsunamis have suggested that some small islands are actually safer than bays or coves as the waves pass around them rather than focusing energy into an enclosed bay. Karangniki lay boat-like with its bow pointing into the swells and hopefully can ride through them to safety.

Typhoons may be another hazard although they rarely visit this area being so close to the equator. Generally, low lying islands and atolls more towards the mid latitudes are very vulnerable to such events.

In a book, *Atolls of the Sun*, an early South Seas traveller Frederick O'brien, retold a first-hand account from Hiram Mervin of a huge typhoon that swept the low lying atoll of Takaroa, part of the Paumotus island chain, seven years before his visit. These islands were for hundreds of years known as the Half-drowned Islands, the Dangerous Islands and the Pernicious Islands reflecting their danger to sailors but also their exposure to storms.

The warning signs for this storm were a gale from the east which had whipped the lagoon to froth. The swell steadily built to huge proportions sweeping over the outside reef and into the lagoon. Soon the surf began to reach towards the edge of the vegetation and the islanders knew a typhoon would be upon them within hours.

Hiram's father told him to scale four huge palm trees that stood near each other and cut their tops off to form a base for a crude platform of planks. They climbed up and waited.

Other sturdy palms were the refuge of villagers able to climb. They sat like birds perched in the upper fronds with the coconuts, hanging onto to what they could. The weaker inhabitants gathered in crowds on high ground. Even at its highest point the island was only metres above sea level. Little children could not climb and they huddled with their parents awaiting their fate. Those at the top of the trees were often no safer as the trees began to sway wildly in the wind. As the sea rose water from below the atoll was forced up through the coral rocks and sand all over the island from below making the islands sand mushy and dough like. It seemed as if the island itself would sink into the depths.

The full force of the storm hit in the darkness and those few out of the reach of the highest waves heard, more than saw, the destruction and screams of people being swept away as endless waves and storm surges covered the island tearing off buildings, palms and people. The sea rose so high that some people were plucked directly from the tops of trees by terrifying waves. It seemed to Hiram that all the devil fish and sharks of the sea were let loose in the night to swim across the island and take his people away.

Next morning after the storm had eased the destruction was revealed. Centuries of bones in the cemeteries had been washed from their graves and strewn about among the stripped bare coral and also in the lagoon. These were mixed in with so many new corpses that the survivors would not fish or dive in the lagoon for a long time. Life on the island had to begin again as it possibly had many times over in the past centuries.

The idle dream of the armchair traveler of living on a tropical island has proven may times over not to be matched by reality. Life on the many tropical islands scattered around our oceans can offer a high degree of sameness under the oppressive incendiary sun. My brother once commented after spending a week in Fiji on a small resort island that he felt a little stir crazy after a day or two and that if he had to live there permanently a thousand years ago he would probably start eating people too!

I understood his point but am a more attracted to tropical islands. Beachcombing and the sights, sounds and experiences of the ocean have a much stronger appeal for me. Also, the variety of life and circumstances for various islands is much more variable in traditional times than one would assume at first glance.

Centuries ago, the local inhabitants understood this well and were aware of the many and varied islands and peoples in their vicinity. The Tahitians knew and visited the Paumotus nearby who were themselves familiar with the Solomon islands further distant still. In *Atolls of the Sun*, a local islander referred to the distant Solomon Islanders as wealthy compared to his poor people on Paumotus. Their wealth lay in the island's geomorphology, where as a product of volcanic action, the Solomon Islands had mountains, deep valleys, rich soil, excellent water supplies and abundant foods such as bread fruit.

On the low lying atolls, the soil was poor, water supplies uncertain and typhoons were a mortal hazard. In their view, the sole advantage they had over their wealthy neighbors was the presence of numerous protected lagoons - safe havens for fishing in all weather. The islander noted that without such lagoons the Solomon Islanders were forced to venture into the open oceans to fish, vulnerable to the feared, long blue shark that was known by islanders across the Pacific, to attack canoes spilling their occupants into the water.

One island was not the same as the other. Life in many islands could have been a dreary struggle with limited water and food in oppressive heat. Others had food, water and space aplenty.

It was common across the Pacific for nearby islands to be in endless wars with each other. The sight of long canoes with paddles flashing in the sun with each stroke heading towards your village could often mean a raid with a desperate fight to the death. Being eaten was a possible outcome.

The motivations for such battles are the same ones that litter our history books with tales of war and pepper Europe with fortified castles. Plunder, revenge, kingly egos and even boredom, are everywhere the sources of most conflict. In less fertile island chains seeking additional protein from a human source also played a role. War could almost be a form of inter-islands sport at times.

A writer once lived with active central-american head hunters only mid last century. He observed the lead up to a raid on a village across in the next valley. The build-up was over weeks as the men and boys raised their excitement levels to fever pitch. Revenge from

reciprocal raids over generations was their stated reason
for the attack. But the writer came to view the event as
more a form of savage sport, a break from the
monotony of their life in the jungle than anything else.

This type of perpetual conflict was not everywhere
across Oceania but was common enough for The
Friendly Isles to be so named because early sea captains
singled them out as naturally good natured and not
warlike. In contrast, the Solomon Islands were feared
for a long time by European visitors as they seemed full
of very large, dangerous and unpredictable inhabitants.

Another outcome of isolation and sameness was the
flowering of innumerable forms of decorations to adorn
both men and women. I once flicked through a battered
old book full of rare early photos of islanders from
across the south pacific before western culture and
missionaries had arrived. There was an astounding mix
of masks, huge headdresses, tattoos and body
decorations made from mud, wood, feathers and other
materials. Many would be familiar to us all. Others I
had never seen before and perhaps are lost totally to
history or exist solely as remnants in a dusty museum
cases and specimen draws.

It seems that a natural tendency for humans in small
isolated communities is to go a little strange - to
decorate, to invent and follow the whim of an influential
chief into weird or wonderful cul-de-sacs of body art
and fashion. Many early European travellers returned
home to the horror of their families with full face
tattoos after going a little too native in the South Pacific.

What seemed a great idea on some faraway isle one day left them with a lifetime of prejudice and embarrassment in their homeland of England.

Much of this flowering of culture and adornment was quickly lost after the arrival of traders, missionaries and colonisation. Missionaries were a particularly powerful force sweeping away many beliefs and practices in their rush to save the poor brown people from hellfire. But, interestingly, Arthur Grimble observed the greatest cultural tragedy for the Gilbert Island communities, where he lived for 30 years, was the arrival of the humble radio. Within years of its presence, the islanders seemed addicted to its babble and ancient beliefs and traditions that had held despite the best efforts of the missionaries, began to fade visibly within years of the first radio's arrival. Decades later, another traveller observed a second wave of cultural destruction across the pacific when videos came to island life and violent Hollywood characters such as Rambo became far more powerful cultural influence than local traditions or the elders.

Of all the Pacific Islands, Hawaii seems most blessed during the centuries before Europeans arrived by an ideal topography, climate, bountiful food, cultural sophistication and a degree of isolation from conflicts. The climate is a touch cooler than the oppressive equatorial regions. The islands had appealing and diverse topography providing coastal living and inland valleys with moist cooler micro-climates. Food was abundant from plants and the ocean leaving much of the day free to pursue recreational pursuits such as sex and surfing.

Both these activities were raised to art forms.

Surfing in ancient Hawaii was part of the fabric of society. It was a passion and a proving ground for warriors and chiefs. The early missionaries were horrified when the surf came up as all the population seemed to stop working and go and ride the waves. They worked hard to eradicate the sport and almost succeeded. Work was good, religion was good but fun and pleasure were seen as the work of the devil.

I may be biased in my view, but I believe that the addition of surfing to the Hawaiian culture in near-to-ideal conditions, must have added a whole new dimension to life many other island cultures lacked. It would have broken the sameness of life in the same way it does for modern surfers who are endlessly intrigued and forever looking forward with anticipation to the next day or the forthcoming swell.

The southern shores of Oahu had powerful surf but also, unusually for a volcanic island, long shelving reefs in the Waikiki area, creating gentle waves that were ideal for learning to ride waves. In the same bay, more challenging waves existed further out to sea and in the peak season for south swell, large waves could be tackled. The Hawaiians had a surfing arena that suited progression and building a novel plaything into a serious sport. Surfing evolving over centuries to the point where even the huge waves of the north shore were ridden by experts on their carved wooden boards.

In recent times many modern Hawaiians have carved

replicas of the old Alaia boards and proven that they can do relatively high performance surfing on them. They are very fast and can be ridden in the tube and do many of the modern turns we are familiar with.

Many surfers could readily imagine giving up all modern luxuries and technology to head back in time to pre-European times in Hawaii to live the coastal life and ride waves on a daily basis. Abundant time, food, surf and the safety of a spiritual relationship with sharks sounds rather attractive.

Historically, in the Mentawais, life for the locals does not seem to have ever been one of Hawaiian abundance. Surfing, in modern times, has become the sole exception. With many of the locals now surfing and an amazing playground on their doorstep, there is a sense that at least something good has come out of their contact with western culture. The fun and laughter of the local children surfing tiny HTs after school on most days is proof of that.

Clive M. Woodward

## 8. FELLOWSHIP OF THE SURF

**Evening – Paul, Coops and... spot the Tasmanian**

Overnight we had moored somewhere new protected behind islands not far from Karangniki. We were up and away quickly the next morning and back to the island for our third day in a row. On the trip over it was clear that the swell had dropped a bit. Most unsettling though, was that there were already two boats there before us. This was a clear sign that nothing else was working back at Playgrounds. We had all become used to being the first boat at every spot we went to, meaning that for a while at least it was just our fellow tourists sharing the waves. It was a bit discouraging to think of crowds and smaller surf for the day. No-one was getting ready to hit the surf this time as we motored into the mooring spot. It all looked too much like a crowded spot at home.

The point was still working and looked to be head high on the sets. The sets, however, were not very frequent and only had 2-3 waves with nothing breaking in between. There were eight people out already. We all sat and watched and pondered our options. Books were read, lap tops opened, smokes rolled and cuts inspected. It was nice for a while just to sit and do nothing after non-stop surfing for days. For me, that feeling of relaxation lasted about ten minutes. I became edgy. Sitting at a point break watching other people surf was not something I find easy to do unless I have already surfed myself silly. It is just too rare a situation for me to be in to switch off and read a book.

A new source of amusement emerged. The boys had spotted a female on the small boat over nearer the break. Binoculars came out and were passed around. My guess was that she was Brazilian given the G-string. She definitely was not shy or demurring. She stood on full display for everyone on three boats to observe for a long time. Guys buy expensive cars, climb mountains or surf 50 ft waves to get noticed. No such effort or stress was needed for this girl. All she had to was don the G-string and stand there.

Tim took a very keen interest. Soon he monopolised the binoculars completely. His tunnel vision was at last working in his favour as he made a detailed study of her landscapes and vegetation.

With Tim hogging the binoculars, my thoughts turned back to the surf. One option existed that offered some hope. The left over the other side of the island was never mentioned in anything I had read on the internet about Burgerworld and so I was skeptical but interested when some of the boys came back after sighting waves there on a walk around the island. Reports on just what sort of wave it was were not clear. I kept asking "what is like". No-one seemed keen to surf it. Descriptions were vague. It was short said some, but Tim mentioned that it peeled a fair way, and was quite a long wave. In the end, I really had no idea and decided I needed to check it out first hand. Charlie was keen for one last surf and made ready to come along. Tim said he just had to go to the bathroom for a bit for a "comfort break" and might follow later.

Charlie and I headed across in the tender with low expectations. We went around the sand spit on the leeward shore of the island and got a real surprise. There was a left breaking from three quarters of the way out along the point for around half the length of the island in total. It was super glassy being totally sheltered from the light wind that was ruffling the faces of the waves on the other side of the island. The look of the waves was just like a Crescent Head in Australia. Long walls peeled off the point and well out into the bay. The colour of the water made it look as though most of the wave was over sand bottom.

Charlie and I were soon in the line-up alone just looking at each other in amazement as a set of quality waves peeled past us and kept peeling for over 200 metres into the bay. This was the left with no name? This was the left that did not rate a mention by the Skipper who knew the islands very well? A set swung in and Charlie caught the first wave and disappeared into the distance. Soon after, I caught one as well – a good workable wall. Charlie stayed in a bit from the most outside takeoff spot and I paddled out near the rocks hoping to get one for the full length of the point. In honour of Charlie I named it C-land.

It was such a picturesque place to sit and enjoy the morning with the island background and the aqua blue, glassy, sand bottom look of the waves. Best of all it was empty. We soon learned it was not quite perfection. The setup is a bit variable in how the waves hit the reef and sand. Some sectioned and others peeled very evenly. A few peeled from the outside peak for a long way down the point. The biggest sets sucked out below sea level in a line at right angles from the point hinting that in a big swell it might be a heavy wave on the takeoff.

Charlie and I picked off some nice waves. Soon Tim joined as and then another few guys from the other boats who had noticed that we had not come back. The spread out nature of the waves meant that no-one really got in each other's way at all. Tim picked up a few waves from where Charlie was sitting. Charlie caught more than a few to make the most of his last surf before heading off to Germany.

Back in Australia such a break would a local favourite no matter where it was located. I would have happily spent a few more hours in the water but sensed that everyone wanted to move on, so headed back with Charlie to the boat. We went around the seaward side of the island.

The crowd had left and just Skelts was out on the right wondering why no one else from the Addiction wanted to surf (now) uncrowded waves.

We arrived in the beautiful harbour just near Telescopes in late afternoon. The swell was tiny and there was nothing around to surf. So we hit the Bintang early moored in the Bay, took team photos and had an early T-shirt presentation.

Charlie awarded the T shirt to me for being ever ready to hit the surf, for my professorial expertise on things Mentawain and for my thorough efforts in preparing for the trip.

Surfing is an amazing sport with variety, thrills and nuances that hold surfers enthralled for years and even for a lifetime. But is can be hard to extract the peak experiences from days mixed with disappointment, crowds and fickle waves that are typically far from perfect. Surfing has always waxed and waned as part of my life with cycles of interests, fitness levels and wave quality. But, there is still little else that will get me up pre-dawn in cold Tasmania or have me run over the sand dunes like an excited kid or make me confront danger in far off locations at 50 years of age. With age, it becomes harder to find things that are exciting and really absorbing. Surfing remains something that still offers so much: excitement, fear, challenge, beauty, fun, the thrill of the hunt, exploration and a touch of the mystical.

Now only nine intrepid adventurers remained as we travelled southward in our own little bubble of reality

pursuing as ephemeral treasures from the sea -
temporary gifts that accepted our admiration and
presence before melting to nothing.

**The Author at Macaronis**

# 9. CRYSTAL GLASSWARE

After a long motor down the coast, we had ended up moored in a bay not far from the fabled Macaronis for the night. I woke predawn and sat up on deck peering into the dark and trying to again sense whether there had been any increase in the residual swell that had gently rocked the boat overnight. Nothing much seemed to have changed.

I headed down for breakfast and drunk my usual 3 full glasses of water to the point that my stomach sloshed with liquid and cornflakes so that there was no chance of getting dehydrated if the surf was good.

We then motored around into the bay. Everyone was up on deck checking out the situation – such was the reputation of Macaronis. The swell was small. Not much was breaking on the right at the tip of the bay.

Sadly the fabled left looked tiny. It was very disappointing given our high hopes. There were no boats in the bay but two dark specs already bobbed in the water indicated that some early risers from the shore camp were out already.

We pulled up next to the break and studied the surf. The guys in the water waved but must have felt anything but happy to see us arrive. Some small but perfect knee high waves were peeling along the reef.

* * *

An amazing feature of the spot is that it is perfect from knee high to double overhead at all tides. This is extremely unusual for a reef break. It means that the ideal sloping bottom has to be there for a very wide section of reef. The bottom there is not a neat, smooth reef like some Australian sandstone set ups. It has dips, holes and channels cutting it up. But amazingly these don't seem to matter as the overall contour as felt by the waves as they hit bottom is perfectly sloped and angled. Swells arrived deep in the bay and have, by then, settled into long lines. They also come in from roughly the same angle so they all hit the reef at the same ideal angle.

The wave itself starts out very hollow and then shifts into a rolling wave that rarely sections. You can turn up and down the face and almost not even look to see what the wave is doing as it just stays the same.

On the last trip we had two days there with 3-5ft surf. Mostly it was 2-3 ft with stray bigger sets. I spent about

ten hours in the water all up over two days and lost
count of the waves I caught. They were small to
medium waves but every now and then I picked up a
wide bigger set. Every time you paddled for one there
was a sense of excited anticipation as a great ride was
certain.

* * *

Soon a small crowd was in the water - us. I paddled in
to the inside, swung around and caught a little waist high
zipper. It promptly sectioned off ahead and I was
caught well behind in the white water and left standing
in knee deep water. Not a good start. I shifted across
to the main takeoff and joined everyone else in picking
off a few small fun waves. Then after we had been in
the water for ten minutes or so, a larger set lined up
across the bay and we all paddled like mad to pick one
of them up. That set the pattern of the day. The dream
waves were scarce. In between were very good but
small waves.

The big sets were the real prize and we were all hunting
them hard. We shared these around pretty fairly
through the day among those sitting at the outside take
off. Tim, Hoover and Paul hung inside a bit where the
take-off speed required to get into the waves was a little
slower.

It was a great surf with long fast rides that were quite
hollow outside and had walls allowing turns up and
down the face and occasional cutbacks. The photos of
the day show Dean on some of the biggest sets in the

pocket and carving on the face, Taff in the pocket in tube stance and slashing cutbacks, Skelts carving off the bottom, Tim soul arching, Paul turning off the top, Doug tucking in for tubes, Hoover trimming in Pugwash Hat and Coops surfing like a young man.

That evening we went back to our mooring of the previous night and looked forward to the usual evening routine of a superb meal, Bintang and good company.

Clive M. Woodward

# 10. GREAT WHITE TUBE HUNTER

**Dean in familiar surroundings on a coral reef**

I woke up on day eight with a now familiar mix of hope and pessimism for the surf that day. We were still moored just around the corner from one of the world's greatest lefts and there were no other boats around that we knew of. However, the forecasts predicted the run of small swell to continue and overnight I was sure the tiny little swell lines that made their way into the shelter of the bay had dwindled to almost nothing.

With the vast Indian Ocean providing a swell window from below Western Australia around to South Africa it was easy to keep hope alive for some new swell. But I was not very confident as I went down to tuck into some breakfast.

Out on deck fellow tourists were up and about but generally looking a little low on energy due to the shared sense that the surf prospects for the coming days were looking a bit average. As we left the bay and headed out around the pint to Macaronis the verdict was clear. The swell had dropped overnight. Conditions in the bay were perfect. There was no wind and the water's surface was glass smooth. A solid swell would have been so perfect it hurt to think about.

We zoomed right up to the point and looked down on two surfers from the land camp out enjoying the occasional knee to waist high waves that came though. On their own they would have picked off some good rides and very occasionally a bigger set would have come through. But with ten of us it would have been a circus. We idled there for a few minutes but never dropped anchor. The decision was made to head to the open coast to check out more exposed spots.

The two surfers in the water had politely waved to us on our arrival, probably through gritted teeth. They waved much more enthusiastically on our departure. We had made their day. They were left in peace for a while to enjoy miniature perfection.

The next stop was to be a fun wave down the coast that was mostly overlooked as too soft and boring for the younger surfers visiting the Mentawais.

From the back it looked small as waves often do. Taff, Tim, Hoover, Paul and I hit it straight away. It was a great option for all of us in different ways. Tim and

Hoover were keen to have a wave with a more predictable take off suiting a longer board. Taff and I wanted to have another go at a fun right and hopefully look for some lips to hit. We all got what we wanted. It was a lot of fun and bigger than we expected. Some well overhead sets came through with a good peak on the takeoff followed by a short wall allowing a couple of turns.

Dean headed over to a left the other side of the Bay we now call Honky's. At first, before the swell dropped a bit, some of the outside peaks were just amazing. They reared up like Pipeline in Hawaii into a serious glassy cobra shaped peak that pitched over into a barrel. It looked very surfable for about 20-30 metres. Then out of nowhere a section would throw over on a shallow spot that seemed often to have no exit point. The peak was so dramatic and photogenic that we all kept looking over whenever a set hit. It was so close to being one of the Mentawai's classic spots, but had a fatal flaw.

Dean sat on a second section as the big outside peak must have been out of the question – otherwise we knew he would have been onto it. The photos that night showed him getting a few waves and a bad wipe-out in very shallow water.

Doug and Skelts came out on the right and picked up some nice waves. Coops briefly appeared later and caught a couple and then went back to the boat. Tim found his spot and began to catch a lot of good waves with his confidence was growing by the minute. Paul was all over the medium ones. Hoover did his usual trick and headed well out to sea to reconnoiter the break with his telescope and depth sounder and seemed about to drift back to the Addiction powered by the offshore wind catching his Pugwash hat. However, as mentioned earlier, he surprised us all by somehow catching one of the sets of the day with a superhuman paddling effort from 50 metres out the back. I eyed the lip off every chance I got. Finally, on my last wave, I dropped in from a deep takeoff spot on a big set and looked up at a long wall with a threatening lip and went straight up really high hit the lip and dropped straight down in a way that was very familiar but I had not done quite so well for a long time. It felt like a welcome visit from an old friend.

Taff and I were the last to head back to the boat and were pretty tired after a long session with lots of waves. The Skipper seemed keen to head for Thunders next as it was a swell magnet and handled the current wind well. We all settled back for the trip, reading books, snoozing and watching the world go by as suited our tastes and state of mind. I was stuffed from the surf and went into the cool of the cabin to sleep.

Only an hour or so later, the Addiction pulled into the lee of the corner of the island around which Thunders peeled. Fellow tourists emerged from their cabins to reconnoiter the scene.

Two boats were already moored nearby and a solid crew of at least ten surfers were out enjoying clean, but inconsistent 4-6 foot waves. It was a long walled left peeling around the corner of the island lined with ancient coral reef and boulders. The shoreline was thick with huge piles of dead trees and driftwood – residue from the tsunami of two years before that had hit the island hard. The tropical jungle previously went all the way to the water's edge. Now it was set back 50 metres beyond the tangled stumps and bleached trunks of the dead palms and other trees.

**Tsunami destruction**

Thunders looked reasonably straightforward from a distance, although it was more walled up and hollow than the videos I had seen of it. Descriptions of the wave always mentioned that everyone gets caught inside at Thunders and ends up on the reef at some point. The Skipper later mentioned that as it gets bigger it moves out into deeper water but on swells this size is quite fast and hollow. From a distance, the main issue for me was the crowd. The guys out there knew exactly what they

141

were doing and were taking off way inside and not leaving much for the more cautious ones sitting wider.

Surf etiquette in the Mentawais meant that we had to hang back a bit and wait for those already in the water to have a session before hitting the water. So we killed time while Geni went over for a surf. He did not get many waves reinforcing my view that it was going to be hard work with three boats on the break.

Taff and Tim decided to go exploring on the Island and so I joined them on a trip into a sheltered little beach nestled between coral outcrops. A few weathered old outrigger canoes were pulled up in the bushes and a path in the bushes suggested that there might was a village inland. I had heard reports that this had been wiped out in the tsunami. The fish net strung off the beach made it obvious that they were still living there.

We walked along the rocks in incredible heat. The contrast from the boast to land was dramatic. The driftwood piles were amazing. The huge jumble of full grown palms and other trees stretched in a line above the high tide mark into the distance. The lush coconut groves lining the coast were now gone. The trunks had weathered quickly in the hot tropical sun and were all bleached to white or a soft yellow.

I took my chance to collect some cowries and the really pretty tiny shells that littered the beach and little inlets along the rocks. Tim and Taff wandered about taking photos. The plan had been to walk along and watch the waves from the rocks. The heat and endless piles of driftwood clogging our path put a stop to that idea.

Walking back to the pickup spot, I stopped to play with some interesting driftwood and began poking long stakes of yellow weathered wood into the base of an old blackened tree stump at interesting angles. I created a little sculpture of sorts to make my mark on the landscape in a subtle way. There was so much raw material you could have made some fantastic works or art with a bit more time and energy. Perhaps my design planted a seed in one of the island's inhabitants and one day I may come back to see a forest of weird driftwood sculptures along the island's foreshore.

We sat in the shade of a palm tree and talked and drunk the cans we had brought along. The heat sapped our energy and the cool of the cabin back on board and more cold drinks became far more attractive than Dante's inferno. We signaled to be picked up and left the island to its heat tolerant inhabitants.

Back on board it was all fairly quiet and the surfers from the other boat were still out there monopolising the waves. I wandered into my cabin for a read that quickly turned into a snooze.

When I woke up Dean and Doug had hit the surf taking advantage of a drop in the crowd level. I watched for a bit and did not see them getting many waves. Surf faded from my plans for the afternoon. In the back of my mind though was the nagging feeling that I should be out there.

The Skipper also headed out for a surf and I became even more edgy. However, I had sort of switched off the motivation tap for the day. Later on Tim went in the boat for a closer look and sent back a message for us to get out there as it was looking good. Evening was not far away, some nibbles came out and a Bintang appeared in my hand. The window of opportunity for a late afternoon surf slipped away. It was my only bad decision of the trip as the photos of Doug and Dean that night revealed all too clearly.

Geni took some great shots of backlit waves with Dean in the pocket and in the tube of solid waves. Doug was caught dropping into some sizable lefts and rode them deep in the pocket with the brilliant green waves framing him. They both came in saying it was one of the best surfs of the trip. Taff and I listened glumly to their descriptions of excellent but heavy waves.

Fortunately there was always tomorrow and we were pleased that one of the other boats had packed up and left. The photos made it pretty clear that Thunders was a heavy wave. Just how heavy I was yet to find out.

The plan for the next morning was to have a quick look around some neighbouring breaks very early and let the other boat have a surf first as apparently they were going to head north leaving Thunders to us. A quality right called Roxys was nearby and I was keen to surf there if possible.

It was Tim's turn to award the shirt that night. We had talked over the candidates early on the island during our stroll. At the time Dean was emerging as a likely candidate. He had tackled the seriously dangerous Honky's left that day and put himself in harm's way in every surf since we arrived.

We need a theme though so Tim could use his artistic skills to do a cartoon of Dean to fit the award on the T-shirt. It was not hard to think up. No one else on the trip but Dean had tried so hard to get tubed on wave after wave, yet failed. We had seen live in the water and in the evening photo shows: Dean locked in the pocket; Dean sticking his head in some whitewash; Dean getting clobbered way too far inside and Dean trying to squeeze his ample frame into tiny Macaronis tubes. If there was a little lick of frothy white water near the top of the wave Dean would stick his head in it. He kept telling us after each surf how he *almost* got a tube. Up to that point, however, Dean could more aptly be termed The Great White Head Dipper: brave, determined, but just not quite up to it. He was like Scott of the Antarctic in the tube department - the glorious failure.

On the island walk earlier we decided we would give the T-shirt to him anyway for sheer effort pursuing tubes at the expense of his mental and physical health. Little did we know that not long after our discussion he would decisively break the hoodoo spell with the tube of the trip, getting perfectly slotted deep in a barrel and coming out cleanly – all caught on film. This was followed up by other tubes on the inside section at Thunders unseen by the camera but described in detail that evening over Bintangs. As I learned the next day this inside section was sometimes perfect hut often just sucked dry and was not to be messed with. Every tube in there deserved retelling.

Tim, therefore, had the amazing prescience to choose the award for Dean and come up with the new moniker: The Great White Tube Hunter (GWTH), a good hour before he had even hit the surf at Thunders. The timing was perfect.

The evening drifted by pleasantly enough but I had a few nervous flutters after hearing firsthand about Thunder's power from Dean and Doug and knowing that the line-up was one of those setups that pushed you into the reef not down it. There was no safe part to the wave. The outside takeoff was right in front of a straight section of reef and the inside wrapped around to face the shore squarely again and was very shallow. The easy fun of Macaronis was over and serious waves were coming our way tomorrow.

**Dean about to exit the tube of the trip**

A Surfing Adventure In The Mentawai Islands

# 11. HEAVY WATER

**The Author at Thunders under some heavy water**

Dawn of Day 9 found us motoring off to explore a couple of other options near Thunders leaving the other charter boat to surf on their own. The atmosphere was humid, with morning mist cloaking the low hills of nearby islands. It felt warm and tropical but mist made it look cool and temperate.

We headed first of all to Roxys, an excellent right that had caught my attention in a couple of Youtube clips. Unfortunately the swell was just too small. Small knee high lines pushed onto the reef in un-surfable rumbles along the exposed coral shore platform. It was clearly a good set up, just the wrong day.

It was an easy decision to head back to Thunders which upon arrival was looking very similar to the day before –

solid 4-5 foot but with long waits and often only 2-3 waves in each set. The guys from the other boat had it well covered. Three of them sat way inside picking up the best waves from there often tube riding the first section and then cutting back to set up the fast inside speed run. The rest were sitting a bit wider picking up the stray wider ones. It looked good but thin pickings if we all headed out there.

We sat and watched for about an hour. In the end I got ready quietly and headed over to see what I could pick up. Initially, I sat inside the wider guys but outside the inside take-off. Close-up it looked powerful but manageable but to sit over on the inside take-off meant you would be faced with a long, fast section straight away. My backhand was feeling good after all the lefts we had surfed and I was confident on making the takeoffs as they were nothing too radical. But my backhand tube riding had hit a snag. It was not so much technique as confidence and fear.

Back in Tasmania in the local beach breaks, in preparation for the trip, I had pulled in to quite a lot of tubes over the summer and knew I could get inside okay and had the tricky twisted stance roughly right. However, the wipe-outs I had on my backhand in the tube seemed to be pretty rough and my board was always just nearby tumbling next to me. The chances of going up and over the falls backhand were much higher than in a forehand wipe-out in the tube. At a heavy left beach break at home I had pulled in cleanly but ended up going completely over the falls head first into shallow sandy water – not something recommended on shallow reef breaks.

All this played on my mind as I looked at the first few waves at Thunders peeled past. Technically I could make the take-off easily and even pull in, but mentally I was not feeling ready for it. Macaronis had been a different story two days before. It was smaller and so perfect that I pulled in tight plenty of times and picked up some nice pocket rides and one tube.

So I sat a bit wider than I could have and waited. A few sets came with the young guys catching each one and zipping past me in the tube. I started to chase anything and finally picked up a pretty small wave between the sets. It all seemed straight forward – drop down, cautious bottom turn then a brief trim and then a turn up to the top of the wave as I had done over and over at Macaronis. It all went wrong. As I was coming off the top the wave suddenly sucked out and next thing I knew I was slammed face first in the shallow water in front of the wave. I popped up, briefly touched bottom and was on my board paddling to get out of trouble. I punched through a couple of walls of white water and scratched over the shoulder of a medium sized set.

"Mmmmm" I thought, "Not a good start."

I waited again without much coming through to catch. Finally, another one came my way. I paddled hard and scraped over the ledge into a very steep take-off on a wave that was going to peel super fast. I should have left it alone but was getting a bit desperate to get a wave. I dropped down sideways in control in a semi freefall and hit the bottom hoping for the best. I landed it but I got blasted again into the impact zone. The immediate impression of Thunders was that it was much more powerful than Macaronis and very shallow just in from where the wave broke. It was too shallow to duck dive so I sort of paddled head first straight at the white water and tried to keep my ground. Two or three waves went past before I snuck out and sat feeling a little shaken. For a moment I was thankful that it was so inconsistent. If it was pumping I think you would have to accept getting washed in and walk around the point to get out again.

The power of the waves was daunting. It was clearly a notch up from Lance's Lefts. The swell was more powerful and the reef shelved faster. The angle they hit the reef made it almost a certainty that you would be caught inside every time you wiped out. Waves also hit the reef sometimes with a wide section that could either give you the ride of your life or shut down on you very easily.

On my third wave I finally picked up a safe one and rode along checking out how it peeled along the reef. It was an easy wave but with a lurking sense of power. The inside section built up and for a split second I contemplated heading into it when all of a sudden it just pushed straight into a super shallow section of reef and became a surge over rock rather than a peeling wave. I pulled high and floated over the back and paddled fast for deep water.

"Crikey" I thought, "You don't want to go near that section on the smaller ones".

By that time Dean, Taff, Skelts, Coops and Doug had reached the line-up. Dean of course paddled way inside. Doug sat a bit wider benefiting from his experiences of the session the previous evening and Taff, Skelts and I hung a little wider still checking it all out. Dean picked off a wave but was caught behind the section and ended up standing in shallow water on the reef. Doug caught one and Skelts and Taff picked up their first smaller waves as well.

The young guys finally left us in peace to head back to their boat. Now there was just Dean in their spot and I moved over closer to him. I chased a few sets but it was tricky to be in the right spot. I paddled hard for a few that went too wide and others wouldn't let me in. I was getting a little frustrated. Then a really big set came through. Dean was in the spot to take it from about 20 metres inside me but would have had to paddle like a demon and it was swinging wide. He looked over at me to see what I was doing. The look from Dean said: "Go Clive and don't pike it as I have let you have this one".

I put my head down and paddled hard as I had learned they often back off a bit and can be hard to get into. I did not look left or right to see what I was in for – just straight ahead. It was the first proper set that I had been in a position to catch after a good 30 minutes in the water and Dean had given it to me – not a time to back out. I steamed over the ledge into a very steep take off. It looked a long way down. I reached the bottom on an angle and after a little sideways drift was soon flying along the wave at top speed. Things happened fast after that. The huge wall stretched forever down the point. I had a flash of that image and then was covered in white water for a split second thinking it was all over. Next thing I was out on the clean face again looking at the cylindrical curves of one of the more remarkable long barreling lefts I had ever caught. It offered the speed run of a lifetime and, for a moment, I thought I going to slip into the pocket and get an amazing ride. Then a thick powerful lip landed just behind my board and the explosion tossed me up in the air and I was rolled and slammed around into shallow water.

I popped up and watched Taff swan dive on the next wave to join me in the impact zone. At that point I had no idea Geni was on shore taking photos and thought my dramatic wave was unrecorded. Even so it was burned on my mind forever, photo or not. A guy from the other boat paddled past and commented that the wave just kept coming at me and would not let me go. I'd made a huge take off, felt safe for a second, was swallowed by white water, escaped that and then finally on its third attempt the wave managed to grab me. That evening I got a real surprise that there was a sequence of the wave and wipe out leaving me with a couple of great shots of one of the heaviest waves I have ever caught. It made the wipe-out and another round of punching through heavy lines of soup over the shallow reef water well worth it.

After that I caught a mix waves and surfed them all pretty cautiously. I didn't push any turns too hard due to the sudden shift in power and suck the wave could spring upon you at any moment and was very wary of the inside section. I caught one other big set with a wide open face later in the surf that allowed a carve off the top and a cutback. It was a great wave that seemed solid at the time. I was surprised to see it was actually double overhead in the photos that night. We were all acclimatised to the size after a week in solid surf.

The photos of the other guys showed that they were doing much the same. Taff picked up one big one and made it right through. One of his best waves ever kept growing as it went down the line. Coops sat in a bit chasing waves like a young grommet and caught some excellent walls. Doug picked off some big ones. Skelts sat a little wider and picked off some of the medium and bigger ones that hit the reef over that way. Dean sat way inside getting some great long waves and some over the falls take offs that left him on the reef.

The sets stayed very inconsistent and, even when the other boat left, it was often a long wait between waves as we shared 2-3 wave sets amongst six if us. I caught some excellent waves in a long session but the quantity was low compared to what I like. My best waves actually came the next day.

We hung out on the boat over the afternoon watching the occasional set of wind ruffled lefts peel empty down the reef. The side shore wind hit the outside section the most but really it was the massive wait between sets that kept me on the boat. Sometimes it was flat for 20 minutes. The size had not dropped much. Eventually in the late afternoon, after seeing one of the biggest sets all day come through, Dean and I headed out for another surf to just see what would come our way. Skelts came out too after a little while and Doug and Taff followed. We all had visions of a late glass off and hoped the swell would kick a little.

Dean paddled right inside as always and beckoned me over. I stayed a bit wide on the hope that the occasional big set would come my way. The bigger ones had been swinging wide. Skelts stayed near me perhaps thinking I knew what I was doing. I did not. The hoped for big sets did not come through and one that did caught me out of position. The surf passed with not many waves caught at all by anyone. The best part of the session was looking at the amazing colours of the green translucent backlit lips as they threw over into space. I almost had to go in without even catching a wave. As dark approached I felt a little bit uncomfortable being in Tiger Shark territory at dusk and was pleased to finally catch a wave and head back to the boat.

Tim, Paul and Hoover had been very patient watching Thunders for a day and a half from the boat. They were itching to get back up to softer waves for a surf more suited to their boards, tastes and bodies. Thunders is just a tough wave to surf. Not every wave was heavy, steep or as dramatic as say HTs tends to be. Some waves were fairly straightforward from start to finish. What was different about Thunders was that the power level was a solid notch above most other spots and it was unpredictable. A wave could sudden shift from routine to a sucking monster or an incredible fast peeling zipper in the blink of an eye. The inside section could be a closeout slam on one wave and peel straight through on others. The smaller inside ones were not a safer option.

They were more likely to get you into trouble than the bigger waves.

That evening we soaked up the atmosphere of another tropical night. It was great that the other boats had headed north and were most likely to stay north as they would soon have to head across to Padang from up that way. The next day offered our last full day of surf. An end of trip feeling started to settle upon us all. We had a great run of surf to look back on and had really made the most of the swell on offer.

The star of the night was of course Paul. He won the T-shirt for a host of reasons. First of all he had emerged as our friendly Doctor Paul courtesy of a huge medical kit and a strong interest in first aid and the elegant spinal board. His authority as a medical expert was enhanced by his general calm and learned manner and his habit of wearing a stethoscope around his neck and a white coat for most of the trip. Dr Paul also took a vital interest in all our digestive tracks especially after a particular curry on Day 5 that loosened us all up. It was touching that even our gaseous and liquid emissions were of interest to Paul's medically trained mind. As a fellow tourist it really did feel as though we had a doctor on board which was re-assuring as we took risks over sharp coral reefs.

Paul also shone out in the surf. He was a selective surfer who knew exactly what suited him and waited patiently for those sessions and then made the most of them. At Bintangs, Burgerworld, Macaronis and The Cut he transformed into an aggressive wave catcher and solid, stylish surfer.

I could totally identify with Paul's approach. Sessions at Bintangs and Burgerworld rated right up there with the bigger days at Lances Lefts and Thunders.

The plan for the next day was to surf Thunders and then cruise north. Everyone was happy with that plan and so we sat back in the tropical warmth with a sense of contentedness that came from having 9 days of excellent surf under our belts and a couple empty sessions to come tomorrow.

**Paul**

Clive M. Woodward

# 12. PARTING GIFTS

**Dean on a glassy morning at Thunders**

The ocean softly shone in the morning light unruffled
by wind. It lazily rose and fell in a silent pulse as swells
passed under the boat. Thunders was peeling away in
the distance, starting well around the point where it was
way too fast, before it wrapped around a curve in the
island towards the main break. Eventually it swung into
the bay and moved from a wave to mind surf only, into
a fast peeling perfect left. The sets were quality waves
and were a similar size to the day before but only arrived
every ten minutes or so. We were in for some long waits
as the in-between waves were just a short ride into a
shallow reef. Fortunately, The Addiction was the only
boat again.

It seemed as if we had been surfing the same long
distance swell from the start of the trip onwards. The

size had slowly dropped and the gaps between the sets gradually increased as the days passed. Over the last four days the swell had not dropped in size. But the waiting just got longer and longer. At other spots this may have mattered less as the smaller waves could provide some fun. At Thunders they were still surfable but the shallow reef cut short the rides. The sets were both much higher quality and safer.

We hit the water after a quick breakfast hoping as always that a new pulse of swell might arrive miraculously to increase the number of sets rolling through. The waves were excellent when they arrived in lonely twos and threes. The faces were pure glass, with ruler edged crests lining up down the reef. Their beauty masked their raw power – until you took off. Between waves, we sat in the early morning heat dangling our legs in the sunlit water and watched the small trigger fish swimming in and out of cracks in the reef. I would gaze in at the tangled pile of bleached tree trunks lining the shore and imagine the tsunami surging in over the island only eighteen months before. The rest of the time, we sat silently lost in our own thoughts and stared out to sea, watching for, and then as the time began to drag, wishing for, a set to come our way. The waits were always long, sometimes ridiculously so.

When some lines swept in from around the point there was a scramble for position relative to the waves and fellow tourists. If luck came your way you would be in position for a powerful fast wall that would speed down the point. The contrast between the peacefulness of the wait and the intensity of the rides always came as a shock. You almost had to shake yourself awake from a daydream when a set arrived and paddle fast just to get the body moving and ready to handle a vertical drop and fast peeling wave.

Not a lot of waves came my way but gradually as the surf wore on I picked some excellent ones. Two waves in particular stood out as up there with my best waves of the trip. Both were a race from start to finish with a fast outside section I only just made and moved straight into a speedy inside section. I was in and around the pocket the whole way.

The photos that night showed Dean in another nice tube and doing a classic cutback on an open face. Doug picked up a big set with huge wall. Coops did a stylish Pizza Man stall in the pocket of a barreling left. Taff caught a perfect one with not a drop of water out of place. Other than that all I saw was the usual back on view of Taff, Dave, Doug and Dean disappearing into steep drops and then popping over the back way down the line. All the dramas and fun lay hidden by the smooth backed tubes of water that rolled shoreward.

This was more comfortable surfing for us all. The waves were now familiar and so clean and perfect that they were easy to ride. Even so they could still swat you like a fly and put you on the reef in seconds. Dean of course found this out a few times by sticking to the furthest inside take off. Geni caught a classic shot of him standing in knee deep water facing a wall of water with no good option to escape. All he could do was jump into it and try not to tumble.

As the morning wore on everyone gradually drifted back to the boat with a nice selection of waves under their belts. I was again left alone in an empty Mentawai reef break. The sun was beating down by now but my trusty blue hat kept me cool. The long waits and fairly short paddles between waves meant that tired arms were not an issue. Compared to a Queensland point break with the constant current or a beach break with a heavy shore break, it was a breeze to stay out for hours. The issue was more staying awake as the gaps between sets could be so long.

As the line up emptied I started to catch more waves and, as had happened on some other days, this gave me more energy and began to wonder whether I should do a marathon and spend a few more hours in the surf or head back to the boat. I was enjoying the surf more and more. I suspected, however, that plans were afoot for a move north. A sense of guilt set in.

I caught a wave which ended with me deep under the lip briefly before I pulled through the back. Geni caught the under the lip shot perfectly. I then sat out in the line-up pondered my options. It felt like the last surf and the trip was over. I was not hopeful for waves anywhere else as Thunders was extracting the last drops from the dying swell. Another hour seemed about right.

The decision was soon out of my hands. I paddled for a steep fast medium sized wave and at the last minute pulled back and was partly sucked into the impact zone. I managed to escape out the back and was swimming holding my ground waiting for my legrope to pull the board out through the back when the strong steady pull on my leg went slack. My legrope had snapped.

Somehow my board popped up only 10 metres away just outside the impact zone and so I swam hard for it. For a moment it seemed like I would get lucky and snatch it from the jaws of the reef. But another barreling wave swept past me and my board disappeared toward the jagged rocky shore. My surf was over and my board probably destroyed.

I waved for the tender to pick me up and was dropped onto shore around the point and started walking out to hunt for the board. Then I saw Geni strolling back with it under his arm. As I got closer I could see three fins still intact which was a relief. When Geni met me I was amazed to inspect it and not find a scratch anywhere. He said it had washed straight in towards where he was sitting in the shade taking photos and he had picked it out of a rock pool. I was stoked!

Next stop was Bat Caves some hours north. We arrived to find choppy 2 ft dribbles across a very promising reef fringing a small island surrounded by steep sandbanks and topped by a tangle of greenery and the ever preset coconut palms. Tim went fishing with the Skipper and had couple of hook ups but no fish landed, Doug and I paddled over to the reef, Doug on Tim's longboard, and me on the SUP, to catch a couple of waves for the novelty factor and had a wander around the island. I found some huge bamboo poles in the driftwood pile and planted them deep in the sandbank lining the shore so they stuck up high into the sky in an impromptu sculpture.

Later on Hoover and a few others went to the island to capture some tropical sunset shots from land. Their comment on my sculpture was a little disappointing. They couldn't appreciate the artistic merit and reckoned it spoiled a couple of their photos.

We left on dusk and Bintang time arrived. A somewhat subdued bunch sat around reflecting on the trip as we headed back to the Lances Lefts area for one last shot at some waves the next morning. With the swell all but gone though it felt like the surf trip was over and, except for a handful of waves at small and extremely inconsistent Lances Left Dean, Taff and I caught the next morning, it was.

Thoughts of home mixed with recollections of an amazing 10 days of surf, fun, good company, funny stories and great food. The days seemed blurred together, each special in their own way. Not a day was wasted and we had made the most out of a good swell that peaked early in the trip and faded as the days went by.

That evening Taff was presented with the T-Shirt for his fine set of abs and 10 days of charging whatever came our way and an incredible tally of cutbacks. Taff was like a martial arts expert working on a perfect high kick. He rolled the move out again and again on his forehand getting more precise and technically correct each time. The arm and head would lead and he would carve it around with control, style and power. On his backhand his cutbacks were a bit more dramatic and radical and a little less graceful. In among the cutbacks there were of course off the tops, bottom turns and pocket rides and the mega wall at Thunders to top it off.

**Taff carving**

The next day the T shirt passed to Tim to wear home in honour of his all round Indo Man metamorphism. On the boat he was good company, a talented musician and provided a slice of life outside the mainstream. In the surf he had a cool mellow style and the tanned presence of a veteran Indo traveler. Tim surfed a path literally blind to exactly where the dangers lay. I doubt whether anyone else has ever done that in the Mentawais before. We all knew that the T-shirt would be in good hands with Tim and take pride of place in his surfing mementos.

**Tim - Indo Man Styling**

**Tim tropical dreaming**

On reflection, my main point of comparison for the 2012 Tour was my previous trip. In terms of swell I think the 2010 tour probably featured more swell. Who could forget the set we watched steam through late one evening at HTs with over 20 waves that lasted for 2 minutes? The stretch around Telescopes and Icelands was a lot bigger last trip. It was virtually flat this time around. However, strangely, I rode way more waves with size on this tour. The solid day at Scarecrows two years before looked only a bit overhead in the photos. Whereas in 2012 Lances Lefts and Thunders had shots of us surfing double overhead waves. I think our best days of swell in 2010 were somewhat wasted by us at HTs where we did not make the most of them. We would have been better off at other spots.

Somehow in 2012 we extracted an incredible run of solid surf from a fairly inconsistent medium-sized swell that slowly faded as the days passed. We had the size early at exposed spots and found it again at the end of the trip at the wave magnet - Thunders. We used the swell magnets when needed keep the run of surf going.

Back home I mused over my favourite surfs and ended up with no particular order. Rather they fell into two categories: the fun ones and the exciting ones. For pure fun, Bintangs, Macaronis and Burgerworld topped the list. The waves were fun and allowed for low risk hotdog surfing. At Bintangs I had a huge wave count as it was fairly consistent and a lot of the time it was mainly Taff and I sitting on the peak picking and choosing waves. Burgerworld was my Queensland point break teenage daydream without the crowds. Macaronis let me surf a left differently to how I had ever done before.

For excitement there were HTs, Lance's Lefts and Thunders. HTs and Thunders both had some of my best waves but were topped by Lances Lefts for sheer length, size and wave count. It is hard to beat a wave which allows you to do 4-5 cutbacks on a two hundred metre wall at speed.

We were very fortunate not to encounter other charter boats much as they would have changed the character of the surfs we had so much. There was never the consistency to handle much more than 6 or 7 people in the water at one time. I like to catch lots of waves! But also the mood of the surf just feels different with a bunch of young surfers in their prime sitting inside having the pick of the waves. The tension rises and the chess game begins. One boatload of aggressive surfers would have ruined most surf sessions we had. I often thought that despite the isolation and many surf spots in the Mentawais we trod a very thin line between having the time of our lives and frustration. Fortunately timing and luck fell our way.

This time around we had the fantastic opportunity to have the best moments recorded by Geni in photos. In over 35 years of surfing I had accumulated only a handful of photos of myself in either classic waves or doing solid turns. Surfing has been like an art form that has been wiped clean the moment I finished my work. Often, the shots I expected to look good in the past were disappointing. The waves always looked smaller and the turn softer.

This time around the quantity of shots was massive but so was the quality. In part this was good waves and being ready to push our surfing but it was also due to the many hours Geni put in siting under his broad brim hat to capture those momentary peak events.

By Indonesian standards Geni was well paid for his long hours in the tropical heat directly by direct contributions by the surfers on board to buy his work. He surfed and by many measures had an idyllic lifestyle. It was only when he made his evening phone call to his wife and young child back in Padang (if we had signal) that you realised the price to pay for such work once a family comes along.

I had more or less resigned myself to never having a good record of my favourite pastime and was so pleased to be proven wrong.

The trip was more than just surf. It was a shared adventure with old and new friends. To sit out in perfect surf in tropical paradise with old mates without a care in the world but which wave to catch was a total pleasure. Old times were shared again and new stories told. The friendships and easy compatibility were unchanged by years, events or distance.

It was also great to meet new tourists and share waves and beers with them. Shared danger and fun create quick bonds.

I felt very fortunate that somewhat late in life these trips had eventuated. They added spice and more than a touch of adventure to life. Back home, non-surfers sometimes gave me blank looks when I said that I had just spent ten days on a boat and barely touched land. I sensed them thinking, "a bit boring". That is until they saw the amazing photos full of azure blue sea and waves and green tropical foliage. Then they sort of understood. What they could never really know was just how many mini-adventures and intense sensations were packed into those ten days.

The trip back across to Padang was a rude awakening and a huge contrast to the calm weather over the past weeks. It rained heavily and a solid uneven wind swell buffeted the boat. Mother Nature was reminding us that she was in control and that not to take her for granted. I lay back in my cabin bed fighting off seasickness. As we neared Padang the seas abated and drifted off to sleep with images of perfect surf and tropical paradises playing through my mind.

The trip was over.

The next one beckoned.

Clive M. Woodward

# The Author can be contacted at:

clivewoodward001@gmail.com

**The Author**

**The Addiction**

The Author

Printed in Great Britain
by Amazon

74744285R00109